PRÁH

Karen von Kunes

Everything You Wanted To Know About Czech and Were Afraid to Ask

*72 Discussions of the Czech Language
to Make you Think, Learn and Entertain*

Práh Publishers
1995

Printed in the Czech Republic

Obálku navrhl a graficky upravil Miloš Novák
sazba: Persona, Alšovo nábřeží 4, Praha 1
Vydal Práh – Martin Vopěnka, pošt. přihr. 46,
181 00 Praha 8 v roce 1995
jako svou 46. publikaci

ISBN 80-85809-19-2

Contents

PREFACE AND ACKNOWLEDGMENTS

Everything You Wanted to Know About Czech and Were Afraid to Ask: 72 Discussions of the Czech Language to Make you Think, Learn and Entertain is not a textbook. Written from a non-traditional point of view, it is intended to give insight into the Czech language, history and culture through grammar. Because of its popular-culture approach, discussions are accessible to every reader regardless whether he/she is or is not familiar with Czech. While they may be very helpful to students of Czech, business people and tourists visiting the Czech Republic, these discussions also may be entertaining and useful to those curious about Czech and Czech culture in general. The discussions can be read randomly since they are presented in a free, rather than progressive order. All the discussions but one were originally published as "Czech List" columns in *The Prague Post* between the years 1993 and 1995.

I am grateful to Ky Krauthamer, my editor at *The Prague Post,* for his many valuable suggestions, fine editing and for creating discussions titles. I would like to thank to Alan Levy, the editor-in-chief at *The Prague Post,* for encouraging me to write the weekly column in the newspaper. I also appreciate the comments of Lubomír Sedlák, assistant business editor at *The Prague Post,* and of numerous readers and students.

Karen von Kunes
Harvard University

This publication was partially supported by a travel grant from the International Research & Exchange Board, with funds provided by the US Department of State (Title VIII) and the National Endowment for the Humanities. None of these organizations is responsible for the views expressed.

Learning to Love in Czech

You'll love it! Yes, you'll love the Czech way of "loving step by step." In English, you can love everything from your shoes to your teacher. Not in Czech, where emotion mounts gradually.

If you're head over heels in love, you may say in ecstasy to your lover, *Miluju tě.* That is, "I love you." Please don't be upset if your lover replies, *Mám tě taky rád,* or "I like you, too." Czechs are reserved in expressing their feelings, and they've adapted their language accordingly. In fact, *mít rád někoho/něco (ráda;* for a female speaker) expresses a permanent state of loving and liking someone or something.

Milovat implies a deep emotional commitment, and you should use it sparingly. Use the particle *se* with these "loving verbs" to express mutuality in a love relationship: *Mají se rádi,* "They love each other." *Milovali se celý život,* "They've loved each other all their lives," sounds fine because of the exceptional lifetime emotional dedication the verb expresses. But, of course, Czech is a tricky language. In other instances, *milovat se* means getting down to the real business, that is, "to make love."

Imagine this situation: You've been at a party and you liked a handsome Czech guy. To the Czech way of thinking, you have judged him for the first time or for a limited period of time, and therefore you can only say *Líbil se mi* — literally, "He has been pleasing to me." Next morning, you realize you've fallen for him, so you can safely say *Zamilovala jsem se.* And finally, only after you've become profoundly familiar with him, you may want to tell him, *Mám tě ráda.* What follows next is your own decision. But please use your judgment first — both linguistic and moral.

Wanted Dead or Alive: Czech Grammar

For those of you afraid of dying, the only consolation I can offer is that you'll live forever — at least from the viewpoint of Czech grammar. When your body becomes nothing but a skeleton, *kostlivec,* you'll still be treated like an animate species. What are animate and what are inanimate species? Stick to this rule of thumb: use your brain, *mozek,* but don't use your logic, *logiku.* Alive or dead, all living and formerly living beings — animals, reptiles and insects are animate nouns. Everything else, including trees, bushes, flowers, bacteria, fall into the inanimate category.

How about the parts of your body? You've guessed. Your heart, *srdce,* doesn't live; nor does your stomach, *žaludek,* your eyes, *oči,* your hands, *ruce,* or your legs, *nohy.* Your brain, *mozek,* doesn't count for a living species either; nor your body cells, *buňky.* So what does count? You, as a human being, *lidská bytost;* you as a foreigner perhaps, *cizinec,* and a traveler, *cestovatel,* you as a reader, *čtenář,* and I as a teacher, *učitelka,* and writer, *spisovatelka.*

My eight-year-old son believes in ghosts, *duchové,* and devils, *čerti,* but I don't. While I may or may not accept their existence, I can't deny their animate qualities in Czech. And how about UFOs? In case you haven't updated your scientific knowledge in the field of ETs (extraterrestrials, *mimozemšťanů),* a Swiss parapsychologist has been seriously concerned with the existence of these "Eufonians," *ufounů,* because he fears they've been reducing human IQ. With such an impact on our intelligence, we had better acknowledge their living qualities for our grammar purposes. And when you wonder next time... please don't wonder; remember your brain is "dead," *neživotný,* but you as a whole person are alive, *životný.* And that's what counts.

Of Mosquitoes and Men: Gender in Czech

Unlike people in the United States and other Western countries, Czechs remain largely oblivious to sexism. But before you place all the blame on today's Czech men, take a look at Czech history, culture and language.

You can observe male dominance in some linguistic features, such as the past tense. To illustrate this concept, let me give you several examples. Consider the following statement: *Muži byli v místnosti,* "Men were in the room." You must write "i" in the past participle plural *byli,* because *muži* is a masculine animate noun.

If you change the subject into a masculine inanimate or a feminine noun, such as *počítače,* "computers," or *ženy,* "women," then the "i" *byli* must be changed to "y". The new sentences would read as follows: *Počítače byly v místnosti,* "Computers were in the room," and *Ženy byly v místnosti,* "Women were in the room."

What happens when the two groups mix together, such as men and computers or men and women? Not surprisingly, men win every time. You are required to write "i" — *muži a počítače byli...* or *muži a ženy byli...*

One could perhaps comprehend this male domination as a historical trend, but what is less understandable is the notion of a mosquito or lizard dominating women and girls. The following sentence is an example: *Ženy a komáři byli v místnosti,* "Women and mosquito were in the room."

You could have an army of millions of women and a lone man who was old, sick, crippled and dying, but the masculine grammatical form would still dominate.

And so it goes for a dog, horse, snail, or mosquito — they all determine the ending in the past tense. Recently, attempts were made to unify the endings of all genders. But Czechs are conservative and the proposed changes were rejected.

I hope, at least, the committee that made the decision was composed of men rather than mosquitoes.

Taking Titles to the nth Degree

No one is as proud of titles as the Czechs are. They are particularly fond of their academic titles. Do you sometimes wonder why young people are introduced as *pan doktor* or, if it's a woman, *paní doktorka*? Well, it's because *PhDr.* until recently was a title given to students in the humanities and social sciences who graduated with *cum laude* at five-year colleges, or who reached the first level of postgraduate education in Czech univerisities. *PhDr.* stands before a person's name and should not be confused with the Ph.D. degree which requires years of training at the postgraduate level. *JUDr.* is the title given to graduates who've completed a five-year undergraduate program in law.

A college graduate in economics, engineering, or technical fields gets the title *Ing.,* and would expect to be called *pan inženýr* or *paní inženýrka*. Needless to say, a man who operates a locomotive or fixes your car shouldn't be mistaken for *pan inženýr*. In people's minds, certain occupations are associated with certain titles: for instance, a publisher with a high-school education might be referred to as *pan doktor*. If a person has more than one title, you're supposed to use them all: thus someone who majored in architecture, would be *Ing. arch.*

The most common postgraduate degree is *kandidát věd,* "Candidate of Science." The abbreviation *CSc.,* is placed after the person's name. To earn this degree, a student has to write and defend a thesis — it may take as little as one year to become *kandidát věd*. (This degree, like PhDr., is no longer awarded.) There's also *DrSc., (doktor věd),* and a range of professorial ranks, such as *asistent, docent, profesor*. An honorary degree (honoris causa) is represented by *h.c.*

The Czechs love titles, so don't be surprised to be handed a business card that reads *Prof. PhDr. Ing. MUDr. med. h.c.* Jan Novák *DrSc.*

A Pregnant Pause
Preserves Your Dignity

Poluce, preservativ, pregnantní. What do these three Czech words of foreign origin have in common? If you think of the effect environmental "pollution" and food "preservatives" may have on a fetus of a "pregnant" woman, you're wrong. Very wrong. Your health awareness and empathy for helpless fetuses don't suit the Czech way of thinking. I'm not talking ethics; I'm merely stating linguistic facts. *Výjimky potvrzují pravidla,* "Exceptions affirm rules," applies in this case. It's true that most English words of Latin origin in *-ion* (revolution, operation, organization) translate in Czech with the same meaning, ending in *-ace (operace, organizace), -uce (revoluce)* and *-ice (kompozice).* This is also true for English words ending in *-ive,* such as negative, positive, relative. They translate either as nouns *(negativ, pozitiv)* or as adjectives *(negativní, pozitivní, relativní).* Words ending in *-ant,* such as constant, resonant, in Czech have the ending *-tní* or *-ční: konstantní, resonanční.*

So what's unusual about *poluce, preservativ, pregnantní?* Their meaning: unexpected and provocative. *Poluce* describes emission of semen in sleep. The English word "pollution" has been used in this sense too, but how many of us use it in this way? Czech *preservativ* has an even more distant meaning from the English counterpart. When recently reading about AIDS, a student of Czech missed the point. "What kind of a chemical additive are they talking about?" he wondered. The "additive," of course, was a condom! Perhaps with some imagination, you can understand the condom as an additive which "keeps, preserves sperms." Similarly, *pregnantní* has enlarged its original Latin meaning "pregnant, with child, fruitful." Think "expressive, marked and pronounced" — these are the meanings that have survived in Czech. So, next time think twice before using English words that sound similar to Czech.

Czech Symbol More than His Famous Image

Who is this Švejk you see everywhere, in souvenir shops, in bookstores, on beer mugs? To begin with, he's a character created by Jaroslav Hašek (1883-23), who was a writer, satirist and drunkard; that is to say, a true bohemian. Hašek's *Osudy dobrého vojáka Švejka za světové války,* "Adventures of the Good Soldier Švejk During the World War," known in English translation as *The Good Soldier Schweik,* is a novel in four parts, left unfinished at the author's death.

The name *Švejk* was probably adapted by Hašek from the German *Schwank,* "a joke, fun," or from *švanda,* a colloquial Czech word taken from the German and having roughly the same meaning. Indeed, reading *Švejk* is a lot of fun. Full of adventures and silly stories, the book is a biting satire, stylized in the form of Švejk's provocative and somewhat colloquial and vulgar discourses. Švejk acts the fool — so much so that he's hospitalized for insanity — but in reality he's smart and cunning. His chief tactic is pretending to agree with anyone he's dealing with, in particular Czech superior officers in the Austro-Hungarian army. Through his idiotic, funny, submissive and rebellious acts, Švejk uncovers the absurdity of the decaying Habsburg empire.

But for Czechs, Švejk means much more, for he embodies a national character of passive resistance, *švejkismus.* People say there's a little bit of this non-heroic hero in every Czech. Švejk "gave birth" to additional words such as *švejkovina, švejkiáda,* both relating to silly and absurd situations.

Though for many the character of Švejk is inseparable from his ubiquitous image, the famous depiction of the short, square soldier in uniform wearing a good-hearted expression is owed not to Hašek but to his friend, the illustrator Josef Lada.

These Mistakes Are Too Hot to Handle

"*Žádné chyby nejsou hloupé chyby,* "No mistakes are stupid mistakes," might be famous last words for students of Czech.

I recall a Czech friend telling me that Americans are very open about being gay. After a brief discussion, it became clear to me that my friend *mluví o koze,* "speaks about a goat," while *Já mluvím o voze,* "I speak about a cart," as the Czech saying goes. *Jsem teplý,* "I'm gay," and *Jsem teplá,* "I'm a lesbian," in colloquial Czech are, no doubt, word-by-word translations from the English "I'm warm." A mistake of this sort usually provokes a good laugh in the classroom, but you can imagine the embarrassment it may cause in a social situation. After all, how often do people exclaim in English, "I'm a homosexual"?

Despite the recent findings from DNA research that suggest a genetic origin for homosexuality, many people, and Czechs in particular, would never admit their same-sex tendencies.

The lesson to learn? Please, don't underestimate Czech grammar. You need to be familiar with Czech adverbs and a dative complement impersonal structure to be able to say, "I'm hot," *Je mi teplo* (literally, "It's warm to me"). Once you've mastered the structure, you can produce a range of the same type of expressions: *Je mi zima,* "I am cold;" *Je mi dobře,* "I feel good;" *Je mi smutno,* "I'm sad;" *Je mi špatně,* "I feel bad;" *Venku je hezky,* "It's nice outside;" or *Tady je chladno,* "It's chilly here."

Carefully avoid dangerous literal translations, such as *Jsi/jste teplý?* "Are you gay?" and *Jsi/jste chladná?* "Are you frigid?" as well as dangerous liaisons.

333 More Times, With Feeling

Ř is the most intriguing sound in Czech. "Say ř by pronouncing r and ž simultaneously," is the usual advice grammarians offer in their textbooks. If your attempts to pronounce ř have been unsuccessful, don't despair; just realize it's not you but the grammarians who are ridiculous. Actually, learning to pronounce ř is much easier than you may believe; it takes nothing but extensive practice with a native speaker.

The Czechs are quite proud of their ř. The moment they find out you have a problem with ř, they'll quote this well-known tongue twister: *"Třista třicet tři stříbrných stříkaček stříkalo přes třista třicet tři stříbrných střech."* "Three hundred thirty-three silver sprinkles sprayed over 333 silver roofs."

You may have come across words that have this sound in more than one syllable: *řeřicha,* "watercress," *řeřavý,* "red-hot," *přeříznout,* "saw into two," etc. Don't look in a dictionary under r for a word beginning with ř-; like other Czech letters with a *háček,* or "hook" *(č, š, ž,),* ř is autonomous — in the alphabet it follows the letter r. The sounds *č, š,* and *ž* are not difficult to imitate: *č* sounds like *ch* in English "cheese," *š* like *sh* in "ship," and *ž* like *s* in "pleasure."

Most Czech sounds have equivalents in English but there's nothing like ř. It's unique to Czech and even Slovak could be envious of it. Try to say some more words to see how much fun ř is: *Dvořák, řeka,* "river," *pepř,* "pepper," *třeba,* "perhaps," *moře,* "sea," *říkat,* "say," *říjen* "October."

Ahoj, Allegorical Metal Monster!

You may not speak Czech, but you surely know at least two Czech words: *ahoj* (pronounced "ahoy") and *robot*. They are both relatively recent loan words; *ahoj* is an Anglicism that was brought by Czech sailors into the country during World War I. *Robot,* on the other hand, is an invented word by Karel Čapek, the Czech playwright who died in 1938. In the early 1920s, European and American theater-lovers were introduced to Čapek's play *R.U.R.,* or *Rossum's Universal Robots.* While critical interpretations of Čapek's robot play view it as anything from a tragic comedy of capitalism to an analogy for alienation in modern society, *robot* itself is an old Slavic word that designates various kinds of work. Until 1848 the Czech word *robota,* "corvée" in English and French, was used to denote a vassal's unpaid labor to his master.

Who, then, are Čapek's robots? Perfect automatons with high IQs, they are "humans" without feelings and pleasures. Their only functions are productivity and efficiency. Does this ring a bell? If you've ever mused on this subject, you're not alone: Kafka, Sartre and many other Europeans have, too. In fact, *R.U.R.* was a hit in Čapek's time, and although existentialist speculation had yet to find popularity outside Europe, the concept of "robot" became widespread and the word gained international acceptance.

Robots are the invention of the human mind; Čapek's robots were created by a scientist, Professor Rossum. The professor's name is symbolic enough — the Czech word *rozum* means "mind, brain." I guess Čapek knew what he was talking about.

A Slav(e) to the Word

Is it a matter of opinion or language deficiencies? "The Czechs are slaves," pointed out a woman from Prague, who had been studying English for some time. A group of American entrepreneurs nodded, wondering what she could be aiming at — are American companies providing ruthless conditions for their Czech employees? The discussion went on in a somewhat embarrassing way until someone asked the woman to spell "slaves." On a piece of paper, she wrote "Slavs."

Interestingly enough, English dictionaries claim both "Slav" and "slave" to be of medieval Latin origin, from *sclavus*, which means "captive." However, dictionaries of Slavic languages often treat "Slav" as a word of unclear origin, relating it to *svoboda*, "freedom," or *slovo*, "word."

While we may not be able to resolve the origin of the Slavs, we should be able to acknowledge who they are. The Slavs entered Central Europe from the northeast, and by the 6th century A.D. had spread out and developed "dialects" of the Old Slavic (or Slavonic) language. In contemporary Czech, we call this language *staroslověnština*. From it originated the West, East and South Slavic groups of languages (Czech and Slovak, for example, are members of the West Slavic group). *Slovanský*, "Slavic," is the term referring to all Slav peoples — which include Russians, Ukrainians, Czechs, Slovaks, Poles, Bulgarians, Serbians, and few others. *Slovenský*, "Slovak," pertains to Slovakia, a country that began its independent history several years ago. *Slovácký* is related to Slovácko, a Moravian region whose customs Milan Kundera described in his first novel *Žert (The Joke)*.

Slovinský, "Slovenian," recalls a less fortunate connection. An ethnic group, the Slovenes were formerly part of the Slavic federation of Yugoslavia, other areas of which are now torn by war.

But what about the slaves? Had the discussion between the Czech woman and the American businessmen taken place in Czech, there would have been no hint of slavery. You could hardly throw *slovan*, "a Slav," into one bag with *otrok*, "a slave."

Hus Laid Down the Law
That Czech Spelling Still Follows

There is a tendency to simplify languages, and Czech is no exception. One American professor went so far as to suggest eliminating the "y" after all consonants (excepting *d, t, n,* where "i/y" has a phonetic function), replacing it with "i." His reason was purely pragmatic: It would make it easier for foreigners to learn Czech.

On the contrary, confusion would ensue for foreigners and Czechs alike. How could we tell whether *bílí* meant "he/she is bleaching" or "white"? Similarly, *bil* would have two meanings: "he was beaten" and "he was." Worse, if we ignore the "d," "t" and "n" exceptions, we would end up with *přirození* meaning both "one's genitals" and "being natural."

Fortunately, some simplifications were made in the past that are appreciated to this day, at least by native speakers: particularly the innovations of Master Jan Hus (1369-1415), the great religious reformer and martyr who was burned at the stake for his convictions. Hus turned spoken Czech of Prague into a literary language, purging it from borrowed foreign words, particularly German one. But his most significant contribution was the introduction of modern spelling, based on the phonetic law that one sound should be represented by one letter.

Czech used to — as Polish still does — use clusters of letters to express certain sounds; for instance, "č" was written as *cz,* "š" as *sz,* etc. Sounds not existing in Latin — such as "č," "š," "ř" and "ž" — Hus indicated with a dot, only later changing the mark to a *háček,* or "hook."

Hus also indicated long vowels by using the *čárka,* or "length mark." Thanks to him, we can distinguish "bleaching" *(bílí)* from "beating" *(bili),* or "fifth" *(pátá)* from a "heel" *(pata).*

You'll find everything about Hus' orthographic reforms in his *De orthographia bohemica* of 1414. Provided, of course, that you can read Latin.

Long Live Czech Literature!

Have you seen or read Václav Havel's play *Largo desolato*? It's a great play about the strengths and weaknesses of human nature. Leopold, the main character, lives with two women, Zuzana and Lucy. He *bydlí*, "lives" with Zuzana and *žije*, "lives" with Lucy. That is, he shares an apartment with Zuzana and is intimately involved with Lucy. While it's true that *bydlet* means "to live" in the sense of residence (in a house, a certain town, etc.), don't assume that *žít* means merely "to be sexually involved with someone." Like the English "live," the Czech *žít* has a much broader range of meanings. If you recall Švejk, the funny and pitiful "good soldier" in Jaroslav Hašek's novel, who personifies the Czechs' passive resistance during the Austro-Hungarian empire, you may recognize *žít* in his slogan *Ať žije císař pán!* "Long live the emperor!"

Is Hašek still living? *Ne, už nežije,* "He is no longer living" — a lover of alcohol and the bohemian lifestyle, he died shortly after the dissolution of the empire. Hašek *žil svým psaním,* "lived for his own writings," and he created in Švejk a character who *bude žít,* "will live," in world literature for a long time.

As you can see, *žít* corresponds to English "live" in many instances. Its metaphorical meaning of intimate involvement must be implied within the context. If you miss this subtle nuance, you'll miss the whole concept of *Largo desolato.*

To Know it All

"Do you know what I know?" Depending on what it is you know and what I know, in Czech you'll end up with questions which differ according to a given situation. When referring to knowing facts, you should use *vědět*. It corresponds to the German *wissen* and French *savoir*. So you would say, *Víte, co já vím?* (Do you know what I know?).

Let's make an assumption that you want to know whether I know what you know. If you have in mind your abilities and skills, then you should ask: *Víte, co já umím?* (Do you know what I can do?) You've told me what you know, so I know what skills and abilities you've acquired. But I still don't know what you know in terms of your knowledge and experience. In order to answer this question, you must ask: *Víte, co já znám?* Here, acquaintance with something or someone is a key to the question. A comparison in German and French would be *kennen* and *connaître*, respectively.

Let's suppose you've told me what you know and whom you know, and you still would like to know if I'm able to do things you do (such as swim, speak Hebrew, etc.): *Umíte, co já umím?* (Can you do what I can do?)

And now, last but not least, you'd like to know if I'm acquainted with your general knowledge: *Znáte, co já znám?* (Do you know what I know?). We could have a philosophical discourse on how to say in Czech what you know and what I know; but first, let's stay within the boundries of Greek philosophers: Know yourself! *Poznej sám sebe!* And let's conclude our discussion in the great Platonic spirit: I know that I know nothing, *Vím, že nic nevím.*

Swallow those Vowels

Have you ever tried putting your finger through your throat? If you haven't, try it. I mean, try saying it in Czech, "Put your finger through your throat. "You'll end up with a sentence made entirely of consonants: *Strč prst skrz krk!*

Czechs love to quote this saying when they discover you're struggling with Czech consonant clusters. Historically, these clusters are survivors from Old Church Slavonic, a written language on which contemporary Slavic languages are based. Structurally, "missing vowel" words can be categorized into several morphological groups.

The most prominent groups are masculine words: *škrt,* "scrape of a pen;" *vrt,* "drill hole;" *drc,* "zipper;" *plk,"* chat;" *šplh,* "rope climbing;" and *trn,* "thorn." Words in the genitive plural feminine category are: *vln,* "waves;" *mlh,* "fogs;" *srn,* "roe deers." The masculine past tense forms are: *trhl,* "jerked;" *vrhl,* "threw;" and *zmrzl,* "froze." Consonant clusters in the imperative category are: *strč,* "put;" *trp,* "suffer."

The art, of course, is to make a decent sentence from this pile of words that includes a few verbs and practically no adjectives (except for a very few reduced to a short form).

I came up with the following sentences, which, by no means, are the best sounding: *Blb pln slz mrkl,* which means: "A fool full of tears squinted." *Strhl srst:* "He pulled down animal hair." *Svrhl drn z Brd:* "From Brdy (a wooded region near Prague), he threw down a turf." *Trp drb!* "Tolerate a gossip." *Plž scvrkl:* "A slug shrank." *Vlk zmrzl:* "Wolf froze." *Strč srp skrz krb:* "Put a sickle through a fireplace." *Z vln frkl:* "He sniffed from the waves." *Hrd, šprt krkl:* "Being proud, a crammer burped."

My sentences may seem silly or funny, but they still can't beat the traditional cliché, *Strč prst skrz krk!* They prove that Czechs can form sentences without a single vowel. If consonant clusters are difficult for you, consider yourself fortunate that you don't have to deal with compound words in Czech. I believe a word like *plnhrdšprt* would be a tongue twister even for a native speaker.

Join the Hat Parade! (If you Dare)

To je ale paráda! "What a show!" Well, listen to this: A guy took Czech at his American college and got straight-A grades in all his courses. But when he came to Prague to report for the *U.S. Times* on the guards' parade at Prague Castle, the word *paráda* threw him off.

To begin with, the day before the parade he tried to get a souvenir, a military-style cap. Seeing how recklessly he was handling her caps, the saleslady said, agitated, *"Chcete, abych si vás vzala do parády?"* The poor chap thanked her for the "invitation to the parade," explaining to her that he was too busy (and anyway, she wasn't his type). The saleslady seemed not to mind — she was eager to sell a cap to the "rich" American. She pointed at one, saying, *"Jen kupujte! Copak jsou ty čepice pro parádu?"*

The young man thought he understood every word: She wanted him to buy one, since the caps were for the parade. He smiled — she must have figured he'd be at the parade anyway. *"Nahoníte s ní parády až až,"* she added. Was she saying he'd be "chasing a girl at the parade?" He was getting confused. The only thing he understood for sure was that she wanted 500 Kč for the cap.

It was a bargain; he was about to pay when he noticed a young boy standing behind him. *"Vždyť vás bere na hůl! Ta čepice je jen pro parádu!"* And now this kid! A "stick" *(hůl)* and a cap for the parade? Was he supposed to get both? He looked helplessly at the boy. *"Vykašlete se na čepici, ať má ta ženská po parádě,"* the boy whispered.

At that moment, our valedictorian said in despair, "Do you speak English?"

In case you, too, got straight A's in your Czech classes, here's what the saleslady meant: "Do you want me to give you a piece of my mind? (Literally, but incorrectly, "invite you to the parade.") "Here, buy one! The caps are to be purchased, not to be looked at (literally, "Do you think these caps are for smart wear?")... You'll be more than attractive in this one!"

And the boy tried to warn our American friend that the lady was taking him for a ride ("putting you on a stick") — the cap was good for nothing *(jen pro parádu,* "just a fancy cap") — and he should forget about *(vykašlat se na,* "cough up") the cap so the saleslady would lose on the deal (be *po parádě).*

If you were to master the colloquial use of *paráda,* I'd say, *"To je ale paráda,* or "Gee, that's great." And I'd give you extra credit.

Not Every Bird Flies

There's no bird like a Czech bird. The word for a "bird" is *pták*. In Václav Havel's play *Largo Desolato*, Leopold is saying to Lucy: *Neužívej, prosím, slova milenec... Představuji si pod ním jakéhosi věčně nahého majitele ptáka—*. One could translate this literally, "Please don't use the word lover... I perceive it as a sort of eternally naked owner of a bird." Every year, students of Czech stumble over this sentence: some find nothing wrong with it, others question its meaning. What kind of bird is Leopold talking about?

The Czech word "bird" can be quite suggestive. For instance, a psychologist and author, Eva von Rheinwald, depicted a man using a bird for a substitute of a woman in a story entitled *Ptákovina*. The motto of the story, *Pojď, ukážu ti svého ptáka*, "Come, I'll show you my bird," arouses readers' curiosity.

By now, you might have guessed the figurative meaning of *pták*, especially if you're a woman. Call it female instinct or, in the Freudian sense, the sublimation of female desire, but the fact is that women typically figure out that in both Havel's play and Rheinwald's story, *pták* means "penis." Strange as the meaning may sound, it is not, for even English slang uses animals and parts of animals' bodies for "penis": cock, prick, pecker.

The world *ptákovina*, however, is free from sexual connotations; it describes a situation produced to laugh at someone or something. Eva von Rheinwald succeeded in using both *pták* and *ptákovina* in a funny and evocative context. Similarly, Václav Havel used *pták* in an unobtrusive, free from vulgarism scene.

By the way, Havel's line was translated by the well-know English playwright, Tom Stoppard, "Please don't use the word lover!... It turns man into nothing but an ever-naked prick."

Why Foreigners Spell Czech Better Than Czechs

Let's review a basic lesson for 7-year-old Czech schoolchildren: When followed by a "y" sound, all hard consonants must be followed by the so-called *tvrdé,* or "hard," *-y,* and all soft ones by the *měkké,* or "soft" *-i.* Many adults, even highly educated ones, consistently violate this rule. Curiously enough, however, English-speaking students of Czech make very few mistakes in spelling words with -y/i. To see why, let's continue that second-grade lesson.

First, remember that *-y* and *-i* represent the same sound (like the "y" in "funny"); they differ only in writing. Second, you have to learn the hard and soft consonants. Presented in the order required in Czech schools, the hard ones are: *h, ch, k, r, d, t,* and *n;* the soft ones are all those with a *háček,* or "hook" *(ž, š, č, ř, ď, ť, ň),* plus *c* and *j.* Third, all the other consonants belong in a mixed group. They can be followed either by *-i* or *-y* (or by *-ý/-í;* the *čárka,* or "length mark," makes no difference here).

Take a deep breath if this seems too complicated. It really isn't, and the proof is that most likely you won't make *-y/-i* spelling mistakes unless you're a native speaker of Czech. This is because Czech kids speak the language long before they learn how to write. Non-native speakers, on the other hand, must learn everything from scratch — speaking, writing and reading at the same time. Naturally, they rely on visual memory more than on rules. So they know, for instance, that *byl* means "he was" and *bil* means "he beat."

A Rich Fruit from Deep Linguistic Soil

Zázemí is one of the few Czech words that are hard to translate. It comes from *země*, "land, country, earth," and in a general sense corresponds to the English "background, setting." *Slovník spisovné češtiny*, the dictionary of literary Czech, defines *zázemí* as "a territory lying behind another territory."

Clear enough. But what about the girl who wants to get married because she needs *zázemí*? Or the man who, after leaving his native country, cannot find *zázemí* in his new home? A character in Václav Havel's play *Vernisáž* (The Private View) says little things, such as a good supper, hold a family together and help to create a feeling of real *zázemí*.

To paraphrase Kundera's statement on *lítost*, "grief," you might say that *zázemí* incorporates a feeling bigger than life — it represents everything that makes your life worth living. It's a feeling of security that you have reached, are trying to reach, are afraid to lose or worry that you won't find anywhere else than in your proper environment. It's a combined appreciation of many feelings and values: love, security, ambition, success, your culture, language, family, relatives, friends. It's an abstract notion, though, an ephemeral feeling that comes and goes.

Zázemí is a common word, dear and important to Czechs and used in both literary and spoken Czech. Almost every Czech writer talks about it in a story, novel or essay. One only wonders why dictionaries leave out something as essential as the abstract meaning of *zázemí*. Perhaps it's too complex to be defined — or perhaps it's really bigger than life and simply doesn't fit into a dictionary.

Making up for Lack of "The"

Do you remember "The Donald?" That's what Ivana Trump used to call her husband in the days before Marla. Ivana's habit of using "the" before her husband's name was often attributed to her admiration for him. But the truth is that she, like many other Czechs, tends to use the English articles "the" and "a/an" inappropriately. Article usage is one of the most intriguing — and difficult — aspects of English grammar.

Czech, on the other hand, has no definite and indefinite articles. Thus, "the power," "a power" and "power" translate only as *moc.* You may wonder how Czechs indicate the word "the." Well, what Czech lacks on one hand, it makes up for on the other. The demonstrative pronouns *ten,* "that" and *tento,* "this" can be put in front of almost any noun, particularly in spoken Czech. *Ten člověk, co seděl u toho stolu, mluvil o tom jídle.* Literally translated, this means: "That man who sat at that table spoke about that food." *Ten* must be in the proper gender and case; but it can also be used as part of both formal and colloquial compounds: *tenhle, tento* and *tenhleten.* And if the speaker wants to create distance between himself and his subject or object, he can use *tamhleten, tamten,* or *onen.*

Declension and the pronunciation "dle" of the particle *-hle* is what makes these demonstrative pronouns challenging. Each part of these pronouns declines independently; only the particles *-hle, -to* and *tam-* remain unchanged. Some forms are complex and quite symmetric: *tomuhletomu, tímhletím, tohohletoho, téhleté, touhletou, těmihletěmi.* Other forms are less complex and less symmetric: *tamtomu, tímhle, tamtěch.* So next time you hear *tomuhletomu* or *tohoto,* remember that Czech has no articles — and that in language, rules are not always as simple as they seem.

Go to the Post Office and Stamp Your Feet

While in Prague, I witnessed a funny scene at the Central Post Office. *"Chci dupat"* (I want to stamp my feet), said a young American man to the woman behind the post office window. Laughter followed, with several employees saying, *"Tak ať si dupne* (So, let him stamp his feet)!" I assisted the fellow by asking him what kind of stamps he needed, and explained to him what *dupat* meant. "I found *dupat* in my dictionary," apologized the embarrassed American. I sympathized with him. In fact, the traditional — and so far best available — dictionary on the market, Ivan Poldauf's *Anglicko-český/česko-anglický slovník*, lists about 20 Czech verbs and nouns for the meaning of the English "stamp."

How do you, indeed, choose the right word for a trivial and concrete enough concept like a postage stamp? I, myself, tend to view the dictionary as an evil crutch in learning a foreign language and consequently have discouraged my students from using one. Especially a Czech-English/English-Czech dictionary. To begin with, most of these dictionaries have been created for native speakers of Czech, and don't provide the information one needs for learning the language, such as noun gender, verbal aspect, verbal classes, etc. They also give a list of often unrelated meanings without further comments. This, by itself, implies the need for a Czech-English/English Czech Thesaurus, or a dictionary that would contain not only grammatical peculiarities but also would show, in a simple context, how each word is being used.

The question, of course, is why a work of this sort has not yet been produced. Compiling a dictionary is a tedious job and most scholars don't have enough patience and/or guts to spend endless hours working on something that's not highly regarded as a scholarly endeavor. Meanwhile, I'm afraid, we'll have to be satisfied with what we have: a dictionary that tells us the definition of "stamp" is *dupnutí* (stamping feet), *razítko* (the mark made by stamping), *otisk* (imprint), *cejch* (brand), *stoupa* (mill-crusher), and many others. Even a linguistic genius will have a hard time sorting out this pile of words until a more detailed context is provided. In fact, at the post office you need to ask for a *známka*.

Sexist Slang
Not Related to Gender

There's a Czech song about liking *holky,* "girls" and *vdolky,* a kind of doughnut. Most likely, these two ended up together for no other reason than rhyming: girls have little in common with doughnuts, except that they're usually the ones who make them. Czech men, like men in many other cultures, shy away from cooking, and other typically "female-oriented" domestic chores.

Another kind of Czech pastry are *buchty,* square rolls similar in taste to *vdolky,* with jam, cheese or poppy-seed filling. Unlike the round *vdolky, buchty* look like chubby little boxes and have feminine gender (in the singular, *buchta,* while the singular *vdolek* is masculine). If you agree that women's bodies are more exposed to criticism than men's, you may have guessed how *buchta* is used as slang in this context. Using it as a word for a girl or woman is condescending but not vulgar, it expresses exactly what she is: a homey, usually plump woman who probably likes baking *buchty, vdolky,* and *koláče* (another kind of round pastry). While not extraordinarily beautiful, she is not necessarily unattractive; on the contrary, she can be pleasant and nice, but her personality lacks qualities that attract the user of the term: assertiveness, self-confidence.

Who, then, is her opposite? A woman with a lot of steam. *Ta holka má páru,* you'd say in Czech. She's the sort of woman who gets a head: in her relationships, profession and status. She's like a steam engine that powers ahead, attracting onlookers. A man can also have *pára,* "steam," but he can't be called a *vdolek, koláč* or any other culinary product of masculine gender. But you can use the names of other domestic items to denote his "weak," non-aggressive, household-focused character. Words such as *bačkora,* "slipper" and *trouba,* "oven" (both of feminine gender) imply it all: he's just an "unmanly" man — and that's taboo in Czech culture.

Czechs by the Hundreds

Examine the word "Czech" in Czech in all possible situations and all cases in the singular and plural. In English you'll get two forms, "Czech" and "Czechs", but in Czech you'll get about 100 forms. It's true that some forms look identical, but they belong to different grammatical patterns.

Recently, a student claimed, "It must take longer to Czech kids to learn Czech than it does to American kids to learn English!" No, it doesn't. When I brought my 3-year-old daughter to Prague, she learned to speak Czech at the level of children of her age within 3 months. But if you're older, you must rely more on structure and less on "natural assimilation."

It might help to imagine a "memory box" in which to classify Czech forms and endings. Make a space in the box on the right for *Mluvím česky,* "I speak Czech," *Umím česky,* "I know Czech," and *Rozumím česky,* "I understand Czech." On the left of the box, place *Studuju češtinu,* "I study Czech," *Mám rád češtinu,* "I like Czech," or *Nenávidím češtinu,* "I hate Czech." *Čeština* is a subject; you can study, like or hate a subject, but you can't speak a subject.

Are you proud of your Czech ancestry? When you speak of it, say *Jsem Čech* here. *Čech* and, for a woman, *Češka,* are the only acceptable variants. Place this in the upper right of your memory box and don't embarrass yourself by using the subject *čeština,* the adverb *česky,* or the adjective *český.*

An adjective modifies a noun, so use it with a noun only, like in a sentence: "This is my Czech friend," *To je můj český přítel.* Your lower left of the memory box should retain this information because you want to speak correctly in the Czech Republic. The name of the country, *Česká republika,* is too cumbersome; I've noticed some English speakers have started shortening it to "Czech." But that corresponds to *Česko,* a term that carries pejorative nuances for many Czechs. The language experts at Charles University, however, have decreed that *Česko* it will be, so record it in the center of your box, since the Czech Republic belongs in the center of a map of Europe. After all, you have to make proper connections when learning Czech.

Spelling Out
Gregor Samsa's Secrets

Many people are familiar with Franz Kafka's story *The Metamorphosis,* about a traveling salesman, Gregor Samsa, who wakes up one morning from unsettling dreams to find that he has been transformed into a monstrous bug. Few, however, know the possible origins and significance of Gregor's surname.

Kafka, a German-speaking Jew, was born and lived much of his life in Prague, surrounded by Czech people and culture. Although he spoke German at home, was educated at German schools and wrote in German, he knew Czech and communicated in it, for example with his translator and lover Milena Jesenská. Kafka had a troubled childhood and felt alienated from his family, especially from his strong-willed, if not despotic father. In *The Metamorphosis,* Gregor Samsa becomes totally alienated from his family after being changed into a giant insect. The name Samsa has since become synonymous with anxiety and alienation.

A number of critics have speculated that *Samsa* is a cryptogram for Kafka (replacing *k*'s with *s*'s and *f* with *m*). Scholars have also suggested that Gregor's surname is a phonetic contraction of *sám,* "alone" with *jsem,* "I am." In the natural flow of spoken Czech, which Kafka knew, *sám jsem* does sound something like *samsa.*

Controversial Topics Need Better Translations

The U.N. population conference in Cairo last September made you realize how difficult it can be to translate the political terminology of human reproduction. Just a simple word like "abortion" raises difficult questions, for Czech has one equivalent, *potrat*, for both "abortion" and "miscarriage." You can define which of the two you mean by, for instance, describing abortion as "the artificial termination of pregnancy," *umělé přerušení těhotenství*, or "the expulsion of fetus," *vyhnání plodu*. Medical terminology uses *abort* or *abortus*, but again, put into plain Czech it comes out as *potrat*, which can be either the voluntary or involuntary extinction of new life.

Neither is "sex" easy to translate. The word *pohlaví* is the general term to identify the male or female of a species, but it has recently been used in the sense of *pohlavní styk*, "sexual intercourse," though this remains an awkward expression. The derivatives from "sex" such as "sex education," "sexual health," and other terms like "reproductive health" and "reproductive rights" can also cause a headache to Czech translators.

"Single-parent household" has no equivalent from either the linguistic or cultural viewpoint because Czech doesn't use the singular *rodič*, "parent," although the form is acceptable — perhaps reflecting the social condition that raising a child is the mother's responsibility rather than the father's.

The phrase "empowerment of women " seemed to be the translators' highlight at the summit. With the negative feelings for feminism in the Czech Republic, one can hardly imagine how this notion could be introduced in the language and culture. The word-for-word translation *zplnomocnění žen* simply won't do.

History Through Adjectives

Strolling through Prague, you may admire bridges, squares and buildings while wondering about the origin of their names. Take for instance *Karlův most*, "Charles Bridge," *Karlova Univerzita*, "Charles University," and *Karlovo náměstí*, "Charles Square."

The endings *-ův*, *-ova* and *-ovo* denote the so-called possessive adjectives commonly used for place names. As a rule, possession can be expressed either by the genitive case or by the above endings. With place names, however, you don't have an option of using the genitive case: you can say *přítel Karla*, "Charles' friend," using the genitive, but you can't say *Most Karla* for Charles' bridge across the Vltava.

The possessive adjectives are somewhat tricky because they have a mixed noun-adjectival declension. Czechs feel comfortable with them in place names; in other instances, they use them sporadically, tending to avoid forms like o *matčině přítelkyni*, "about mother's friend;" *k otcovu bratru*, "to father's brother;" etc. These forms not only sound too bookish, but some native speakers may not be sure of the endings (at least in less commonly used cases) because they are used so infrequently in spoken Czech.

If you glance at a map of Prague or any Czech town, you'll find countless uses of possessive adjectives: *Masarykovo nádraží*, "Masaryk's Station;" *Wilsonovo nádraží*, "Wilson's Station;" *Jiráskovo náměstí*, "Jirásek's Square;" *Smetanovo nábřeží*, "Smetana's Embankment;" Králův Dvůr, "King's Court." They also exist in the plural as in *Karlovy Vary*, "Charles' Spa."

Names such as *Václavské náměstí*, "Wenceslas Square" and *Havelská ulice*, "Havel's Street" are pure adjectives formed from personal names and typically go far back in Czech history. Just don't confuse them with the name of the Czech president!

This Expression is Not One to Get Behind

When Czechoslovakia was invaded by Warsaw pact troops in 1968, a prominent politician is said to have exclaimed, *Jsme ztraceni,* "We're lost." "But he would never have said such a thing," well-known writer Josef Škvorecký has argued. "He'd say, *Jsme v prdeli,* " — "We're up the ass."

I agree with Škvorecký. Although one dictionary of American slang advises caution when using this word, and most Czech dictionaries avoid *prdel* altogether, the word has, by and large, crossed over the boundaries of vulgar usage. There are over 30 idiomatic and slang expressions with the word *prdel,* many of them used by educated speakers in both less-formal and semi-formal situations. There's a beauty and power in the word *prdel* — beauty in its richness and power in its usage — that fits the Czech character of resignation and skepticism.

To understand *prdel,* you must savor its flavor. It can mean anything, even fun: *Nedělám si z vás prdel,* "I'm not making fun of you." If you don't like someone, you could say: *Ať jde do prdele!* "Let him go to hell."

There are many myths about Americans; poor or rich, in the eye of Czech beholders they all *Mají plnou prdel peněz,* "Have their ass full of money" — are filthy rich, in other words. But, of course, it's understandable, for they have just been lucky," *Měli z prdele kliku,* being born in a country of wealth. But is it only luck? I see a basic difference in the two nations' attitudes toward work — the Americans respect hard work, the Czechs don't — or did not during the communist regime. *Do prdele práce,* "The hell with work" is a common expression; it can also be used in the sense of "damn it!" or "shit!" if someone isn't succeeding in an effort.

Then there's the disputes, a sort of "gentle revolution," currently going on between Czechs in the Czech Republic and Czechs émigrés. The émigrés *Mají plnou prdel řečí,* "Have their ass full of advice" on how to become prosperous, and some still living in the republic resent them. After all, most of them left the country *s holou prdelí,* "with a bare ass," and now they expect those who endured four decades of communist hardship *že jim polezou do prdele,* "to crawl into their ass," — to follow their advice, to please them or to say nice things to them. Well, maybe it's time to "kick their ass," *kopnout je do prdele!*

Summer or Winter, It's Always Czech Time

Watch your watch! That's the rule of thumb for telling time in Czech. Like the Romans, who used to divide the night into quarters, the Czechs divide the hour into quarters. Except at the exact hour, they look ahead at the coming hour, and manipulate minutes (within a 10-minute span) around each quarter. Thus, 2:15 becomes *čtvrt na tři;* that is, "A quarter of the hour has passed toward three o'clock." 2:23 offers a challenge since you can say it either by adding eight minutes to 2:15, *čtvrt na tři a osm minut,* or by subtracting seven minutes from the half-hour, *za sedm minut půl třetí.* If you need to say "It's 2:40" use either *Je půl třetí a deset minut,* "It's half of three o'clock and 10 minutes," or *Je za pět minut tři čtvrtě na tři,* "In five minutes it will be three quarters of three o'clock."

When you think of it, this method is fun and logical, but has one drawback: you need to visualize a dial watch to see the minutes you must add or subtract at the coming quarter hour; in other words, you must "watch your watch." If you're hooked on your digital watch, feel free to use the "timetable" or 24-hour system. And don't despair if your watch is programmed for the 12-hour system: just add *ráno* (morning) or *dopoledne* (late morning) for a.m., or *odpoledne* (afternoon), *večer* (evening), or *v noci* (at night) for p.m.

The Long and Short of Czech

Look at these two Czech words: *vila* and *víla*. They might look alike to you, but to me they are as different as English's "fit" and "feet." The sound that English indicates by "ee" is rendered in Czech by the so-called *čárka*, "a length mark," over an "i."

And as in English, it's not only the pronunciation that makes the two words different; it's also the meaning.

Vila is a Czech word of Latin origin describing the kind of mansion President Havel bought on Dělostřelecká street; on the other hand, *víla*, an old Slavic word, is a kind of fairy — the type that made Geppetto's wooden puppet Pinocchio come alive. To begin with, do not confuse the *čárka* with an accent stress, as most students do when they begin learning Czech. Interestingly enough, every word in Czech is stressed on the first syllable. It's irritating to listen to Western reporters pronouncing Martina's surname *Navrátilová* with a stressed *lo* syllable. Only the first syllable, *Na*, is stressed, and the two length marks in her name indicate nothing but long *á* as in "father."

But the problem runs much deeper. Again, I have to note that our Czech-learners' rule — *Žádné chyby nejsou hloupé chyby,* "No mistakes are stupid mistakes" — is misleading to the point of embarrassment. Take this situation: A guy is pursuing a girl, but she tells him she has to go. *"Kde máš byt?"* he asks, which means, "Where's your apartment?" She feels harassed and leaves. Only later does he realizes he meant to say, *"Kde máš být?"* or "Where do you have to be?"

Fortunately, other mistakes of this type can lead to situations — in Kundera's terms — of "laughter and forgetting": *hrabě,* a title of "Count," versus *hrábě,* "a rake;" *mile,* "nicely," versus *míle,* "a mile;" *žila,* "she lived," versus *žíla,* "a vein." As long as you understand what the speaker is talking about, you can laugh. It's like the time my 3-year-old daughter discovered that her brother had "peanuts," and she didn't. You and I know what she meant!

Putting Your Foot in It, Czech Style

It may not look like it, but Czechs are obsessed with footwear, and they have the vocabulary to prove it. When you visit a friend's home, for example, you are expected to *přezout se,* "change your shoes," or put slippers on. What kind of slippers? You may be offered a variety of them, such as *bačkory* (soft slippers), *papuče* (warm slippers), *trepky* (light slippers), *pantofle* (open slippers) or *dřeváky* (wooden slippers).

Then there are the names given to sports sneakers, such as *cvičky* (from *cvičit,* "to exercise"), *tenisky* (from tennis), or *kecky* (from *kecat,* "talk rubbish", or possibly from the original sneakers' brand name Keds as one reader suggests). All these are called *přezůvky,* from *přezout se,* where the prefix *pře-* indicates a state of crossing, in this case "changing from one kind of shoes into another." Originally *přezůvky* denoted overshoes meant to protect your feet against rain or snow.

Unless you bring your own to your friend's house, you might be offered your friend's slippers or those of any member of the family as long as they fit you. Seems Czechs have no idea that many people suffer from athlete's foot, jock itches, ringworms and other kinds of foot infections that can be easily spread from one person to another.

Czechs love their shoes, no matter what, and give them all kinds of expressive names. For instance, *lodičky* — literally, "small boats" — are denoting high-heel shoes women "float in" on ancient cobblestone sidewalks of Prague. *Kozačky* are boots that took their name after a particular kind of high boots worn by the Cossacks. The pejorative *bagančata* is a kind of unattractive-looking military-style boots. But no matter what kind of shoes you put on your feet, think twice — especially if the shoes are not yours but your host's.

Be Flexible and That's an Order!

In English, if you say "Mary loves John," it means just that, never that he loves her. If you want John to be the lover, you must make him the subject and put him in his proper place: "John loves Mary." This is callled changing the word order. In a flexible word order, such as in Czech, you can, more or less, place words the way you like them. Thus, *Marie miluje Jana* and *Jana miluje Marie* are interchangeable and convey nothing other than "Mary loves John." If he loves her, you can say either *Jan miluje Marii* and *Marii miluje Jan.* The subject in a Czech sentence is the same no matter where you place it. This is also true for objects and verbs: You can place them almost anywhere, as long as you preserve their required endings.

So, what's the fuss about? It's about Czech word order being one of the most, if not the most, difficult aspects of learning the language. I've met language gurus who claimed there's nothing as intimidating in Czech as the word order. This is because of the little devious words called enclitics.

Imagine them as little dictators standing on top of a pyramid. They are few and seem insignificant, but you can't ignore them. They love two things, rigid order and hierarchy. You can't move them, you can't replace them with each other, and you can't begin a sentence with them. They must be second: the second unit in the sentence or in a clause. In the Olympics, they'd get a silver medal, just like Nancy Kerrigan.

So you must first identify the first unit. It can be any word except *a,* "and;" *ale, ba,* "but;" *i,* "even;" and, naturally, the enclitics themselves: *se, si, ti, mi, mu.* Also proscribed: *jsem,* "am," *jsi, jste,* "are" in the past tense; and a few others. But more often, the first unit is a complex of mutually dependent words, such as *během svého nočního spánku,* "during my night's sleep."

Then you can move to the second step: identifying and rank placing the enclitics, as in *Říkal jsem si to, když jsem se mu na to díval.* "I was saying it to myself when I was looking at it for him." Here, because the sentence is relatively simple, you have only one other possible word order: *Říkal jsem si to, když jsem se mu díval na to.* But I can assure you that in a long sentence, word order can become quite a puzzle.

The Most Valuable Czech Words

To purchase dollars in Bohemia, you have to pay quite a few crownstoday. But there were times when you didn't have to change money to receive dollars. To be precise, as early as 1519, the dollar was, in fact, a monetary unit in Bohemia.

Historical records show that the Czech word *tolar,* like the English "dollar," was borrowed and adapted from German "thaler," which in turn is short for "Joachimsthaler," a silver coin mined in Joachimsthal — "Joachim's Dale" or, in Czech, *Jáchymov* — in west Bohemia.

The word *tolar* has not survived in modern Czech. Used only as a historical term and in old songs and folklore, it has been replaced by *koruna* or "crown" (from German *Krone)*, which originated with old Austrian coins showing a ruler's crown.

The smallest Czech monetary unit, one-hundredth of a crown, is *haléř,* or "heller." This word comes from Old German *Heller,* a small coin minted in the town of Hallu. You may also hear *halíř,* a spoken Czech form of the term.

The various coins and notes are sometimes given one-word names in speech: *desetník* for *deset haléřů,* a 10-heller coin, *dvacetník* for *dvacet haléřů,* a 20-heller coin, *padesátník* for *padesát haléřů,* a 50-heller coin, *dvoukoruna* for a 2 Kč coin, *pětikoruna,* a 5 Kč coin, and *desetikoruna,* a 10 Kč coin or note. Similarly *stovka* is a 100 Kč note, *dvoustovka* a 200 Kč note, *pětistovka* a 500 Kč note, and *tisícovka* a 1,000 Kč note. Slang words are also used: *bůra* for 5 Kč, *kilo* for 100 Kč and *tác* for 1,000.

All these coins and notes are *peníze,* "money." The word comes from the little-used singular form *peníz,* which was borrowed from the German *Pfennig.*

The history of Czech money takes in almost everything these days — except the much-wanted 20th-, not 16th-century, dollars.

Marrying Words Lag Behind Changing Society

In English, when you marry, the same word applies regardless of whether you're a man or a woman. But in Czech, you "take" a wife *(žena)* if you're a man: *ženit se.* A woman, though, "gives" herself in marriage, expressed by the verb *vdát se.*

This giving on the woman's part means more than just giving her body and soul. In old times, even as recently as the last century, a bride was supposed to "give" dowry. This was much more than just a bridal gift — usually it meant everything to equip the newlyweds' household. Traditionally, she moved into her husband's house, where special quarters were reserved for the couple, with the rest of the house being occupied by her in-laws.

There has been progress made since then: Society has became more equal in terms of who "gives" what and where the newlyweds reside. In the communist era, thousands of apartment houses were built all over the country to allow young couples to live on their own. But this didn't change linguistic habits. However, spoken Czech does commonly use an expression that implies more equality than *ženit se* and *vdát se: vzít si za ženu/muže,* "to take for a wife/husband," or simply *vzít si.* And *vzít se,* "marrying each other"has become a 50-50 enterprise even in literary Czech.

The Language's Unbearable Difficulty of Definition

In *The Book of Laughter and Forgetting,* one chapter is called "Lítost," and according to author Milan Kundera, this Czech word has no equivalent in any other language.

He describes the feeling of *lítost* as a combination of many feelings: "...grief, sympathy, remorse and an indefinable longing." *Lítost* "can have a very narrow meaning, a meaning as definite, precise, and sharp as a well-honed cutting edge," Kundera argues. Not finding this sense of word in other languages, he writes that it's difficult for him to comprehend "how anyone can understand the human soul without it."

You could argue with him on at least three counts: First, you could question whether he has searched for equivalents for *lítost* in the thousands of languages and dialects people speak. Second, you might criticize his typically Kunderian, pompous statements and phrases: once carefully scrutinized word by word, they may appear quite pretentious. Third, you could point out that the word *lítost* is used relatively infrequently in Czech.

The use of the word is illustrated by the expressions *cítím lítost,* "I feel sorrow," and *k mé lítosti,* "to my sorrow or disappointment." Much more common than *lítost* are the idiomatic expression *je mi líto,* "I regret, feel sorry," the verb *litovat,* "to be sorry" in the sense of having compassion, and the verbal noun *politování,* "pity, sorrow."

Czech-English dictionaries give the following equivalents for *lítost:* remorse, repentance, sorrow, grief, compassion, commiseration, sympathy, pity, regret, literary "ruth" (referring to a broken heart) and contrition in the religious sense.

You may agree with Kundera that *lítost* is a combination of many feelings but disagree that understanding the human soul may be difficult due to the lack of the precise meaning of *lítost* in other languages. Are small children or mute people free of grief, compassion, sorrow, sympathy or regrets just because they can't express their feelings by words?

It can be argued that the English language is richer and more subtle in expressing feelings accurately by a variety of words than Czech. And Czechs themselves prefer using other terms than *lítost* to describe the feelings that Milan Kundera is talking about.

'Tis the Season for Etymology

Every month, Czech is an exception. Most European languages — including Slovak — base the names of calendar months on Latin. Czech, together with a few other Slavic languages, doesn't, using instead popular beliefs etymologies.

January is *leden,* from *led,* ice. Etymologists agree that *únor,* February, refers to broken ice floating on water; the stem is from *nořit se,* "to float."

Březen, March may be derived from *bříza,* birch tree. March is the time when birches come to bud, and the next month, the oak, *dub,* sprouts — hence *duben,* April. In May, flowers, or *květy,* bloom, and the Czechs have named this month *květen.*

Červená, red is the color of cherries, but it's also a time when *červy,* worms, appear on trees. For the months of *červen,* June, and *červenec,* July, you can choose between beautiful fruit and ugly worms.

August, or *srpen,* is the month of harvest; the name comes from *srp,* or sickle, a tool used for reaping. *Září,* September, and *říjen,* October — when animals mate — derive their names from *(za) říje,* (during) "rutting." Some may, however, find it easier to remember *září* as a month of glitter — from *zářit,* "to glow, to shine."

In November, as nature prepares for winter, leaves fall, *listí padá,* so Czechs call November *listopad. Prosinec,* December, is the month of gray days; at least that's what etymologists believe. *Siný,* "gray, colorless," is the stem in *pro-sin-ec.* But if you make promises and pleas on the New Year's Eve, think of *prosinec* as a derivation from *prosit,* "to ask, to plead."

Languages leave room for flexibility, however. Not only Czechs, but also Poles and Ukrainians think leaves fall in November; Croats think it's in October. It's a matter of cultural differences.

A Word for an Imposing Idea

I need you to help me find a word for "harassment." The lack of its counterpart in Czech has its essence in conceptual and linguistic approaches to the act itself.

What is harassment, anyway? Many Czechs don't — or don't want to — understand it. Take the Czech man, a professor and administrator at the University of Miami in Florida, who sexually abused many of his students and colleagues. In a recent interview on U.S. television, he cried and said he hadn't been serious when he committed his crimes. I wonder how many Czechs are serious about harassment.

In his article in the weekly magazine *Mladý svět*, Vladimír Stwora used the word *harašení* as an equivalent. It's tempting to make this connection, not only because of the deceivingly similar-looking stems *haraš-* and *harass*, but also for the figurative usage of *harašit*, "get crazy ideas." In this colloquial use, *harašit* is condescending and so, by analogy, is the whole concept of harassment. *Komu tam haraší?* "Who gets crazy ideas?" Of course, the person who feels harassed. I say "person," because contrary to popular beliefs, men may feel harassed to the same degree as women do.

When the novelist Josef Škvorecký wrote a series of articles on harassment for *Respekt*, another leading weekly, he translated the word as *obtěžování*. True, harassment is *obtěžování*, "bothering, troubling, disturbing," but I prefer *vnucování*, implying "impose, force" — as in "imposing something unwanted on someone," and that's exactly what harassment is.

We could also use *nátlak*, "pressure," but it seems to me that Czech needs a foreign word to express harassment, a concept that's foreign to Czech mentality. I propose to use *impozice*, "imposition" (similar to *kompozice*, "composition"). Then we could say *pohlavní*, "sexual," or simply *sexuální impozice*.

It's possible the Czech ex-professor in Florida will come up with yet another term; after losing his job and his house, he has learned that sexual harassment is a serious offense — at least in the U. S. But before he reveals his intimate details — and possibly new terminology for harassment — in his promised memoirs, we shall satisfy with *sexuální impozice*. That is, unless you find a more convenient term.

Czech Grammar Case By Case

Don't make a federal case out of Czech cases. True, Czech has seven of them, but in general, they produce less than seven forms of a given noun, adjective, pronoun or numeral — and sometimes as few as two. For instance, *náměstí,* "square," doesn't change at all in the first six cases, and the seventh-case form adds *-m: náměstím.* Keeping track of the cases can be tricky, though, and that's why Czech usually refer to them by number, according to their order in Latin grammar. The Latin nominative case is *první pád,* "first case," the genitive is *druhý,* "second," the dative is *třetí,* "third," followed by the accusative, *čtvrtý pád,* "fourth."

Unlike many other European languages, Czech has an "addressing" case, *pátý,* or fifth in order, which is based on the Latin vocative. Any time you address a person or any other living thing, you should use *pátý pád:* say *Martine!* when talking to your friend *Martin,* and *paní doktorko!* when asking a question of your female doctor, *paní doktorka.*

Only the prepositional (or locative) case cannot stand without a preposition. To the great distress of students, many grammarians present this sixth, *šestý,* case in paradigms without a preposition, which is not only incorrect and illogical but above all unnatural, at least to a native speaker of Czech. This doesn't mean, of course, that all nouns attached to a preposition must be in *šestý pád.* The prepositions *o,* "about," and *v,* "in," do typically require the sixth case, while *s,* "with," is usually associated with the instrumental, the seventh — *sedmý* — and last case."

How do we use all these cases? A very similar way as in English. You wouldn't say, "I know she," would you? So in Czech, you can't say *Znám ona,* but *Znám ji,* "I know her."

Briefly, remember that a sentence subject requires the nominative, or first case. Direct objects take the accusative, *čtvrtý pád (píšu dopis,* "I'm writing a letter") and indirect objects *třetí pád (píšu příteli,* "I'm writing to a friend"). Express possession by *druhý pád (matka mého přítele,* "my friend's mother"). There's more to it than that, of course. Just get on the case.

Mastering Czech More Than a Formality

Like many other European languages, Czech distinguishes between the familiar "you" *(ty)* and the formal "you" *(vy)*. The second-person singular *ty* is used when speaking to someone with whom you have a friendly or intimate relationship, or to a child, while in all other cases the second-person plural *vy* is appropriate.

Children should always be addressed with *ty*. If you're not sure how old a child is, it's safer to use *vy* — especially when addressing a teenage girl. Often finishing their formal schooling by age of 15, many Czech children become self-supporting and should be addressed as adults.

Typically, family members — parents and children, grandparents, uncles and aunts, and more distant relatives — use *ty* with each other. In-law relationships can be tricky — if you feel accepted and welcome in your spouse's family, you can *tykat* (use the *ty* form); otherwise you may be better off *vykat* (using the *vy* form) when talking to your father- or mother-in-law.

When is the proper moment to switch from *vy* into *ty*? It depends, of course, on many factors — upbringing, level of education, and desire to be friendly or intimate with the other person.

It has long been believed that the woman usually proposes, *"Mohli bychom si tykat,"* or "We should start using *ty*." But some people prefer to keep a distance — regardless of how well they know each other — insisting on the *vy* form of address. In some extreme cases, even lovers prefer to use *vy* — as a sign of respect, a verbal symbol of perpetual novelty in their relationship or simply because it's unusual.

But no matter what, politeness is part of Czech culture. Formal situations and relationships always demand that you use *vy*, and no first names.

Accentuate the Negative

Linguisically, if not in their thinking in general, Czechs like to negate. The rule is simple: When you negate, negate everything! Imagine a Czech mother sending her child to camp with this kind of advice: *Nikdy nikam neběhej!* "Don't run anywhere," *Nikoho nepomlouvej!* "Dont' gossip about anyone," *Nic nekritizuj!* "Don't criticize anything," *Nikomu neraď!* "Don't advice anyone," *Nikým nepohrdej!* "Don't despise anyone," *Nikomu neznámému nepomáhej,* "Don't help anyone you don't know," *Nikomu nic neslibuj!* "Don't promise anything to anyone," *Ničeho nelituj!* "Don't regret anything," *O nikom nehezky nemluv!* "Don't say bad things about anyone."

While she — unlike author Jackson Brown who hit "a jackpot" with life rules for his son — wouldn't make a fortune hawking these rules we know she's correct, at least grammatically. Except for the preposition *o,* "about," she negated every word, leading us to expand our rule: Each word that *can* be negated *must* be negated.

Negative words include all negative verbs (formed with the *ne-* prefix: *nepracovat,* "not to work," *nespat,* "not to sleep"); adverbs with the prefix *ni-*: *nikdy,* "never," *nikde,* "nowhere," *nijak* "in no way," etc.; the pronouns *nikdo,* "no one," *nic,* "nothing." Add to these the adjective *žádný,* "no, none," and *nijaký,* "not any sort of," etc. This negating works the same as in English; what's different are the double, triple, quadruple, etc., negations, as in *Nikdy nic nikde nikomu neříkej a nijak se nezabývej žádným problémem.* "Don't never not say nothing to no one and in no way don't bother with no problem." Now that's positive thinking.

Use Pet Names With Affection — and Caution

Diminutives and pet names are a nice feature of the Czech language, and their usage isn't difficult. They don't necessarily denote small people and things, but rather anything that the speaker has a close relationship with and perceives affectionately.

Pet names such as *bratříček*, "little brother" from *bratr*, "brother," *Milánek* from *Milan*, *Alenka* from *Alena*, *Mařenka* from *Marie* are formed by endings *-íček*, *-ánek*, *-ka*, *-enka*, among others.

Besides personal names, diminutives and pet names can also be formed from many nouns, particularly everyday objects: *krabička*, "small box," from *krabice*, *domeček*, "little house," from *dům*. Some objects, such as *lžička*, "small spoon," *hodinky*, "watch," and *milenka*, "mistress," exist only in diminutive forms. Others may have a diminutive ending that does not denote its quality: *halenka*, "blouse," *Zdenka*, a neutral variation of the name *Zdena*. This latter variety may cause confusion, since many female names do take the ending *-ka* to express endearment: *Helenka* from Helena, *Milenka* from Milena, *Olinka* from Olina.

Parents address their children by their pet names; some names may have only one variant, but common names have two or more. So if you name your son *Josef*, you can call him *Jozífek*, *Jožka*, *Pepa*, *Pepíček*, *Pepánek*, etc. Ivana Trump named her daughter *Ivanka*, which would have been unacceptable in the Czech Republic, because birth certificates can only record a neutral form of personal names.

Some surnames like *Beránek*, *Havlíček*, *Havránek* have survived in their diminutive forms and can't be used in any other variation.

The use of pet names is widespread in Czech, but be sensitive, because by using a diminutive you may express more affection than you intended. Basically, any familiar or intimate situation allows the use of diminutives and pet names; you can call your mother *maminka* rather than *máma* or *matka*, your aunt *tetička* or *tetinka* rather than *teta*, and your lover *Petříček* rather than *Petr*. If you communicate with a group of people, schoolchildren for instance, either call them all by their pet names or none. In a context like this, using a pet name for one person and not another implies practicing favoritism.

Saying a Lot With a Little

Nó. Jó? Co! No a... copak? Né! To. Á? Little words that have simple definitions can mean many things. Take *no:* an abbreviation of *ano;* it can be pronounced either with a short *o* or with a kind of long singing *o* sound. Depending on the speaker's intonation, *no* can express anything from happy agreement to an angry interjection. *Jo* has a similar function in colloquial Czech — you can translate it as "Isn't it true?", "I agree, you're right," or "What do you think?" Again, intonation and vowel length depend on situation and mood.

"Is that right? I can't believe it!" can be expressed not only in full sentences (*Je to pravda? Tomu nevěřím!*) but also by words such as *co* and *ne*. *No a* can also express a strong statement such as "So you think I'm a fool? Well, I don't give a damn!"

In a translation, you may struggle with *copak*. It's one of those emphatic words expressing surprise, disagreement, etc., depending on the context. For instance, *Copak to ještě neudělala?* could be translated "Hasn't she done it yet?"

Ne means *"no,"* but in conversation (often pronounced *né*) it has many meanings: "Aren't I right?", "Do you agree?", "What nonsense!"

Without doubt, *to* is a handy word that can fit almost anywhere. *To* really means "it," but is often used in the sense of "this, that" in a hesitating way: *Víš to, no tamto, o čem jsem mluvil...* "You know that, the thing I was talking about..."

The little word *a* connects two statements, but is also used to express surprise, etc., in the sense of "That's interesting," or "Well, what should I do?"

Often you'll find these little words together: *No, a co já?* "Well, and what about me?" The only way to learn all these words' meanings is by listening to native speakers and using a lot of your own imagination.

The Day of Carp and the Baby Jesus

Vánoce, vánoce přicházejí, zpívejme přátelé, — "Christmas, Christmas is coming, let us, friends, sing," are the words of a song from the 1950s. While the song may not be as popular as it used to be, celebrations of Czech Christmas remain as joyful and traditional as in the past.

It's a family event to which friends are rarely invited. The highlight of the holidays is Christmas Eve, when presents are opened, typically after a dinner of fried carp. There's no Santa Claus; *Ježíšek,* "Jesus" is supposed to put presents under the tree on Christmas Eve. But Czech children never see him — he's not personified by a character in a costume like Santa is.

Although Christmas is a religious holiday for only a few Czechs, the word *vánoce,* "Christmas," retains its original spiritual meaning: It comes from German *Weihnachten,* meaning "holy night." *Vánoce* gave birth to other words related to Christmas, such as the adjective *vánoční* and the noun *vánočka,* a big, sweet oval loaf of bread with a braided top. You slice it and eat it with your tea or with a drink after dinner.

You can even buy *vánočka* in American stores. But if you offer it to Czech guests at an inappropriate moment — as my husband once did in the middle of summer with a beef dish — they'll give you a perplexed look. After all, Czechs like to stick to their traditions.

Keep Hat on Head

Which of these statements is correct? "Put your hat on your hat" or "Put your head on your head." You could argue that both or neither are correct. It depends on how you view them — logically, grammatically or phonetically. In this case, I'm referring to Czech assimilation — not of the cultural type, but the linguistic assimilation of voiced and voiceless consonants.

What does it mean? Some final voiced (vibrating) consonants are pronounced as their voiceless (non-vibrating) counterparts. For example, the final "d" in Czech is pronounced the same as "t" (*led,* "ice," sounds exactly the same as *let,* "flight"); "ď" is pronounces as "ť" (*zeď,* "wall," sounds like *zeť,* "son-in-law"); and "z" is pronounced as "s" (*lez,* the imperative of "climb" sounds the same as *les,* "forest"). I can think of many other examples.

Unless their English phonetic skills are superior, native speakers of Czech naturally transmit these assimilation habits to their English pronunciation. So don't expect your Czech lover to say, "I love you," but rather "I lofe you."

If you also consider the Czech pronunciation of English vowels, you will discover other peculiarities, such as the example at the beginning of this column: "hat" and "head." In other words, "head" sounds like "hat" and, on the contrary, a correct-speaking Czech may pronounce "hat" in a way that sounds like "head." That's what is called speaking with an accent.

Do you wonder whether Czechs sometimes confuse their own words and meanings because of phonetic assimilation? Not at all. They instantly recognize the meaning from the context. In addition, words are usually declined by adding an ending, such as a "u," or "em." For example, the Czech word for hat, *klobouk* could become *klobouku* or *kloboukem,* depending on how it is used in a sentence.

Once words take endings after their final consonants, the assimilation rules are no longer necessary.

Language Takes A Long and Winding Road

When you communicate with a Czech person, you may run into a problem of understanding — but not because you don't understand the language.

The difference between Czech and English does not merely arise from different words. It also stems from the arrangement of ideas within a sentence, from the so-called "thought pattern."

Czechs express their ideas differently than native English speakers do, whether within a short statement, a paragraph, or a complex discourse. An English speaker's thought pattern usually follows a straight line of development.

For instance, if you didn't feel well and needed a day off from work, you would probably simply tell your employer so. If a Czech employee feels the same way, he may start by telling the boss about an event he attended last night, about catching cold going there and how tired he is today. Then, he may (or may not, assuming the employer suggests it) ask for that day off.

The reason is that a native Czech's line of thought is not straight, but rather a series of digressions or deviations from a central idea. This, of course, does not mean that the Czech pattern of thinking is inferior to the English one. It is just different. Czechs, on the other hand, may find English speakers too direct, dry, even impolite.

The style of stringing ideas together is so central to a culture's self-image that a native speaker who breaks the digression pattern may be harshly criticized — as happened to Milan Kundera, whose sentences are constructed by a series of logical statements, bared to essential facts.

Names to Know Down on the Farm

In spoken Czech, animal names are sometimes used to comment on the intelligence, maturity or physical appearance of people. *Husa*, "goose," *koza*, "goat," and *slepice*, "hen," for example, are three creatures of feminine gender, grammatically, so their usage applies primarily to women and girls. While these terms aren't flattering, naturally, they don't necessarily have to be rude; in the proper situation, they can work as euphemisms to replace stronger, more demeaning words. You might call yourself a goose: *Jaká jsem to husa!* — "What a goose I am!" — if you do or say something that later seems silly or inappropriate.

Being a *husa* is much more acceptable than being a *koza* and *slepice*. *Koza* implies dullness, silliness, craziness or weirdness. A *slepice* has a small brain and may describe someone judged to be lacking intelligence.

Unlike in English, "cat," *kočka* isn't a metaphor for a malicious woman but for a sexy, attractive and seductive one — and thus a term that some women may take as a compliment and others as an insult. Slangish *žába*, "frog," describes — without any particularly positive or negative undertones — a girl just getting into her teens; if she's younger, she may be called a *žabka*, "little frog." And a smart girl may be called a *opice*, "monkey." *Zajíc*, "hare" may describe a boy of the same age as a *žába:* an adolescent, inexperienced in love.

A clumsy, bumbling person of either sex and any age is *tele*, "calf." If you do something really stupid, you may be called *kůň*, "horse" or *osel*, "donkey." *Vůl*, "ox," became one of the most commonly spoken swear words in the '60s, so much so that it lost its derisive nuance and was, and still is, often used by young people when addressing each other. Maybe you'd be better off calling your friends by their human names.

Easier Said than Written
Literary Czech rarely makes it onto the streets

A colleague of mine, now a prominent scholar of spoken Czech, learned the language at Harvard, came to Prague and understood almost nothing. Is there really such a big difference between written and spoken Czech? Yes and no. As a literary language, Czech fell almost completely out of use in the 17th and 18th centuries, being replaced by German, while the spoken language continued to develop. In the 19th century, when literary Czech was revived, its proponents had to look back to the 16th century for their models, leaving a significant gap between the written and spoken forms of the language.

While spoken Czech is not subjected to the same rigid norms as literary Czech, there are some rules. One of the most common tendencies is to use *v-* in words and compounds beginning with *o-*: *okno*, "window," becomes *vokno; on*, "he," becomes *von; modrooký*, "blue-eyed," is pronounced *modrovoký*. The long *-ý* is often pronounced *-ej: mýt*, "wash," becomes *mejt; být*, "to be," is *bejt*, etc. These phonetic changes do not apply to words of literary style and to Czech words of foreign origin, such as *onkologie*, or *výklad*, "explanation."

Many noun and adjectival endings that students spend painful hours learning in class come to naught when they begin to speak. For instance, *starý známý*, "old friend," becomes *starej známej*, while *s velkými kluky*, "with big guys," turns into *s velkejma klukama*, and *za těmi ulicemi*, "behind those streets," is often heard as *za těma ulicema*.

Think of spoken Czech as a glass half full rather than half empty: It allows greater uniformity and simplicity in endings, particularly in the plural. *Vysoký*, "tall," in the spoken language applies to all plural genders: *muži*, "men," *ženy*, "women," *domy*, "houses," *kola*, "bicycles," while in literary Czech you must distinguish between *vysocí muži, vysoké ženy/domy and vysoká kola*.

If you struggle with the notorious consonant changes, relax! Spoken Czech largely ignores them — at least in the masculine animate nominative adjectival plural: *čeští hoši*, "Czech boys," becomes *český hoši*, while *dobří studenti*, "good students," changes into *dobrý studenti*, and *hezcí kluci*, "good-looking guys," becomes *hezký kluci*. And if you want to talk about good-looking guys in the locative plural, please say *o hezkých klukách*, not *o hezkých klucích*. After all, you don't want to sound like a grammar book!

Fishing for the
Meaning of Christmas

It seems that too often these days we get less for more money, and that goes for Czech products as well, including recordings of Jakub Jan Ryba's *Česká mše vánoční,* the Czech Christmas Mass. For 20 years I listened to a version from the mid-60s. The record had picked up a few scratches, so I purchased a new recording last year. But alas, the power of its music was gone. I'm afraid my family will listen to the old Ryba while eating fresh *ryba,* "fish" *na Štědrý večer,* "on Christmas Eve."

What's the connection between *Ryba* and *ryba?* One is the name of a talented and ambitious Bohemian composer (1765-1815) who lived in poverty to produce great music. He did, indeed, create a masterpiece and his Mass has gradually become a symbol of the Czech Christmas. The other *ryba,* "fish," is an appropriate symbol for the season: Almost every Czech family consumes *kapr,* "carp" on Christmas Eve. But there's more *ryba* than just *kapr.* The Czechs begin their December 24 dinner with *rybí polévka,* "fish soup." The adjective *rybí* may produce various case endings, such as *rybím, rybích, rybímu,* etc., but not *-íz* as in *rybíz.* This word, which means "currant," is of Arabic origin, while *rybí* is an old Slavic word.

But this takes us off the seasonal subject. What counts today is *Ryba* and *ryba,* the beautiful pastoral music and the traditional Czech Christmas meal. Even if their quality may be declining, I hope you'll enjoy them.

Veselé vánoce, "Merry Christmas" to all of you!

A Pre-'89 Comrade Might Prefer 'Count' These Days

Czech society has seen some changes in recent years, and so has the language. While communist terminology has gone into decline, new words have made their way into Czech from English and German — mainly business and technical terms. Czech society has also seen and accepted the return — or resurfacing — of old aristocratic families and their historical titles. I say "historical" because in 1918, President Tomáš Garrigue Masaryk's administration abolished titles of nobility, even forbidding the use of aristocratic prepositions — the Czech *z* and the German *von* — in legal documents.

Since Czechs are now allowed to use titles again, we should know what they are and how to use them. Topping the titles of the upper nobility, *princ* and *kníže* were used by sovereign rulers; both correspond to "prince." Then come *hrabě*, "count," and *baron*. In the past, a count was addressed as *hraběcí Milost*, "Count Excellence;" today, you can address him as *Excelence*. Among the lesser nobility — those whose families had earned a title by service to the crown — belong *rytíř*, "knight," and *šlechtic*, "nobleman."

For our linguistic purposes, the most interesting titles are *kníže* and *hrabě*. As nouns, they share the declension of the "young animal" words. So when talking about a prince and count, think first about the endings of *kuře*, "chicken," or *kotě*, "kitten." They add a *-t* in both singular and plural: *kuřete/hraběte, kotěti/knížeti, kuřetem/hrabětem, kuřata/knížata,* etc.

Today, Czech nobility is fully engaged in professional life, and some members have earned academic and professional titles. When addressing a noble doctor or engineer, use this order: *Ing. Jaroslav kníže z Lobkowicz,* or *MUDr. František princ Lobkowicz.* If you're not sure who's who, simply use *pán*, "Mr.," *paní*, "Ms., Mrs.," or *slečna*, "Miss," but please, no more *soudruh,* "comrade." In the post-revolution Czech Republic, *soudruh* is nothing but a historic title, soon to become an archaism.

Czech Proverbs That Say It All

"Love moves mountains." "He who isn't lazy gets the green." "The early bird jumps further." Do these sound familiar? Knowing a few Czech *rčení*, "sayings" and *přísloví*, "proverbs" can help both your language skills and your understanding of Czech culture.

Common sense is at the root of some proverbs, like the one about love moving mountains: *Láska přenáší hory*. Love has such power that it will overcome all difficulties. *Napřed měř, potom řež*, a word-for-word equivalent, "First measure, then cut", means never act hastily, or "Look before you leap." *Nebuď zvědavý, budeš brzo starý*, which literally means "Don't be curious, otherwise you'll get old soon," also falls into this category; in English it's "Curiosity killed the cat."

Some proverbs are the same in both languages: *Kdo se směje naposledy, ten se směje nejlépe*, "He who laughs last, laughs best." *Skutky hovoří hlasitěji než slova*, "Actions speak louder than words."

One saying, *Pozdě bycha honit*, is difficult to translate literally: *bycha*, an auxiliary *bych* ("I would") of the conditional mood, has been turned into a noun. We could translate this as "It' too late," or "Don't cry over spilt milk."

Don't boast of your knowledge of Czech until you understand this proverb: *Neříkej hop, dokud nepřeskočíš*, literally "Don't say hop until you jump across"— or "Don't count your chickens before they're hatched."

In Václav Havel's play *Largo Desolato*, two paper-mill workers endlessly repeat, *Jsme zvyklí kout železo, dokud je žhavé*, "We are used to forging iron while it's red-hot," or "We must act while we have the chance."

Then there are the sayings that rhyme, such as *Komu se nelení, tomu se zelení*, "He who isn't lazy gets the green," and *Ranní ptáče dál doskáče*, "The early bird jumps further" — and probably gets the worm.

Certain concepts are expresssed differently in Czech than in English. *Lepší vrabec v hrsti nežli holub na střeše*, "Better a sparrow in the hand than a dove on the roof," is known in English as "A bird in the hand is worth two in the bush." Similarly, *Zabít dvě mouchy jednou ranou*, "Kill a two flies with one hit" translates into English, "Kill two birds with one stone."

If some proverbs are "all Greek" to you (or "Chinese" to a Frenchman), they are *španělská vesnice*, "a Spanish village," to a Czech. But as long as we understand each other, that's all that counts.

Pick a Basket of Mushrooms

Do you like mushrooms? Czechs do. Not only to pick different kinds of mushrooms in the woods and prepare them for dinner, but also to use the word *houba*, "mushroom" in various metaphors to express nothingness. Some of these expressions imply both literal and figurative meanings, while others are used only metaphorically. *Být na houbách* literally means "picking mushrooms in the woods" while in the abstract sense it's condescending, referring to a person's pre-natal stage. If you hear someone saying *Mám houby*, "I have mushrooms," make sure there really are mushrooms around — otherwise the speaker may just be complaining about having or owning nothing. And if the speaker is bitter or sarcastic, he or she will add vinegar and sourness to mushrooms: *Mám houby s voctem na kyselo.*

How many kinds of mushrooms do you know? A mushroom connoisseur should recognize at least 30 kinds — he must *znát houby*, "to know the mushrooms." You may know mushrooms but still be ignorant; in another way *znát houby* means "to know nothing." *Je to na houby*, "It's (a basket, for instance) for mushrooms," can describe a real object; in most cases, however, it's a handy expression meaning "It's good for nothing." The Czechs usually get their mushrooms in the forest for free; they cost nothing, as does *hovno*, which can be politely translated as "excrement." In this sense, *houby* is actually a euphemism for *hovno* (or simply, *H.*): *Stojí to za houby (hovno)*, "It's worth nothing;" *Vím/umím houby (hovno)*, "I know nothing/I'm good at nothing," or *Mám z toho houby (hovno)*, "I get nothing out of it."

Imported Words Have Sex Appeal

English words have existed in Czech for several centuries, but the strongest waves began after World War II and the 1989 revolution. Sports terminology has been heavily Anglicized for some time: Just look at such words as *hokej, box, fotbal, badminton, gól, tenis, kurt, rekord, puk* — you recognize them all.

While many new words vacillate in their usage and spelling (*busnissman* versus *byznysmen*, *payroll* versus *pejrol*, *boogie-woogie versus bugy-vugy*), others have changed their spellings to adapt to Czech rules *(víkend, sexapíl, striptýz)*.

You find English everywhere: on your dinner table *(biftek, steak, kečup, džem, puding, whisky)*, on yourself *(pulover, džínsy, zip, bikiny)*, on the airwaves *(džez, pop-music, hit, bigbeat)*. Psychology is becoming a popular field in the Czech Republic, but the words *stress* and *tabu* have been found in Czech for quite some time.

English words can penetrate directly from English (in the past usually from Britain rather than the United States), or sometimes through German *(punč)*, French *(drenáž)*, and occasionally even Russian *(kombajn)*.

Czech endings are common for verbs imported from English *(exportovat, bojkotovat, flirtovat)* and for adjectives *(kokteilový, dolarový)*.

A word like *mrakodrap* is hard to recognize as an Anglicism — it's a so-called "calque," a word-for-word translation of a foreign concept, in this case "skyscraper."

Although today, Anglicisms and Americanisms thickly populate the economic and political sectors of the Czech language and you can use many English words, you may also expose yourself to ridicule or simply be misunderstood. They may look familiar, but use words such as *operace, poluce*, which means "wet dreams," *activita* with caution.

What's in a Name? Grammar!

"Why is your surname different from your father's?" an immigration officer asked as I was submitting my papers many years ago. I remember explaining to him that, unlike my father's surname, mine ended in *-ová* because I was a woman. Czech girls take their father's surname, and Czech wives take their husband's, adding *-ová*. So Czechs know the U.S. first lady as Hillary *Clintonová*.

My friend's name is Martina *Kinská*. The ending *-á* is a linguistic device by which masculine surnames ending in *-ý* are declined as adjectives. The feminine adjectival form ends in *-á;* thus, *paní Kinská, Stránká,* and *Nová.* English names ending in *-y,* such as Kelly and McCloskey, are not subject to this pattern because they cannot be viewed as adjectives (their ending is *-y,* not *-ý*), so they become *Kellyová* and *McCloskeyová*.

You may have noticed that the Czech first lady's name is *Olga Havlová*. The "e" has been dropped from her husband's surname *Havel.* This occurs when masculine forms end in *-el, -ek, -ec,* etc. Similarly, author Milan Kundera's wife had to drop the *-a* before adding *-ová* to become *paní Kunderová.* Supermodel Paulina *Pořízková* has kept the female ending *-ová* when spelling her name in English. That's not surprising: *Pořízek (Pořízka)* is a nickname for a stout man — just the opposite that Paulina represents. Also Martina *Navrátilová* uses her surname in the original Czech form; attacked for her same-gender tendencies, you can understand why.

The Czech Language Is Both Perfect and Imperfect

Ninety-nine percent of Czech verbs come in pairs. Why? Because almost every verb has what grammarians call verbal aspects: perfective and imperfective. They express a concept like that of verb tenses in English, and they have to be used in the appropriate way, just as one would use the present perfect or past perfect in English.

Perfective verbs should be seen as a single action, viewed as a whole with a beginning and an end, either in the past or in the future. Take the perfective verb *napsat,* "to write." *Napsal/a jsem dopis,* "I wrote a letter," means you started and finished writing the letter.

The curious thing about the perfective aspect is that it can't be used in the present, because what you're doing "now" doesn't yet have an endpoint and can't be viewed as a whole. Perfective verbs do have present-tense forms, but these actually express action in the future: *napíšu,* for example, means "I will write." So what do you use if you want to say you're writing a letter right now? You switch to the imperfective member of the pair, in this case *psát: Píšu dopis.* The imperfective aspect has present, past and future forms and expresses action in progress, repeated action (what you do regularly, every day, every month, every year) or incomplete action. If you were writing that letter sometime in the past and haven't finished it yet, say *Psal/a jsem dopis,* and if you intend to write it but don't foresee its completion, you'd say: *Budu psát dopis.*

Many verbs that beginners learn in their first classes are imperfective; you could call this aspect the basic form. Perfective verbs are often formed from the imperfective aspect by adding a prefix: *psát* adds *na-,* as we've seen; *číst/přečíst,* "to read;" *vidět/uvidět,* "to see." Some pairs differ in a suffix: *ztrácet/ztratit,* "to lose," *kupovat/koupit,* "to buy." The type *brát/vzít,* "to take," where the two forms are entirely different, is a rarity.

The concept of aspect shouldn't scare you; just remember that completion is always perfective and can't happen in the present. And if you've finished writing that letter, don't forget to mail it.

When Women Ruled in Prague 5

After the death of the legendary prophetess Libuše, ruler of the Czechs, women exposed to men's ridicule and decided to fight back. Led by Libuše's comrade Vlasta, the story goes, they built a fortress on Děvín, a hill across the river from Vyšehrad. Its name bears the imprint of these warrior women: It's derived from *děva,* "girl" in old Czech (*dívka* in the modern tongue).

The fight that followed was bloody, due not so much to the women's strength as to their cunning. The most seductive girls lured men from Vyšehrad to Děvín, where a whole army of women hid ready to attack. Many men died under the storm of sharp arrows loosed by the women.

This tale has survived in the names of streets under the hill, such as *Děvínská,* "Girls' Street," *U Dívčích hradů,* "At the Girls' Fortresses," and *Šárčina,* "Šárka's Street." The Šárka commemorated in this street name was a shrewd girl who helped bring about the death of Ctirad, a strong young warrior. He found her tied to a tree, and she pleaded for release, saying the other women had bound her. When he freed her and blew the horn she carried, Ctirad fell into the trap as women swarmed out and captured him. His cruel death by torture on the wheel enraged the men, who —led by the Prince Vladimír — then conquered the women and destroyed their fortress Děvín. (In the middle ages, a castle was built on the same hill. Later it was used for artillery practice, and no trace of it remains).

While this story is not particularly encouraging to feminists, it has become a part of Czech mythology, celebrated in literature, song and folklore.

A Little Gerund Is a Dangerous Thing

Ask a Czech friend to translate this sentence using a gerund: "Having learned everything, she thought she was smart." If you're lucky, your friend might have an idea what a gerund is, but it's unlikely he or she'd give you the correct sentence: *Naučivši se všemu, myslela si, že je chytrá.*

Czech, you see, unlike many languages, doesn't use gerunds, at least not in the spoken and standard literary varieties. The gerundial forms are limited to an archaic, highly scholarly, or pretentious style (the author Kundera, for instance, uses quite a few gerunds).

In standard Czech, the place of gerunds is taken by an independent clause, as in *uviděl to a zasmál se,* "he saw it and laughed;" or by *potom,* "then," *zatímco,* "while," *protože,* "because," and other words.

For the record, Czech has two kinds of gerunds: perfective (such as *podívav,* "having looked," *napsav,* "having written," přišed, "having arrived) and imperfective (such as *chodě,* "walking," *vida,* "seeing," and *jsa,* "being"). Gerundial endings confuse native speakers; the perfective ending *-vši* for neuter and feminine nouns simply sounds funny — the word *vši* means "lice."

Some gerunds have survived as phrases on their own, such as *chtě nechtě,* "willy-nilly," *nehledě na to,* "disregarding it," *nemluvě o tom,* "not to speak about it," *počínaje,* "beginning with," and *konče,* "ending with."

If you know everything about gerunds that you've just read, you know more than most Czech native speakers and you probably should stop learning about them. A student of mine once was eager to learn gerunds thoroughly, but when he used them while speaking Czech in Prague, people thought he came from another century or, perhaps, another planet.

Meet Czech Head-On

Hlava is an easy word — feminine, hard, singular. It's a common word and, over the centuries, people have invented numerous metaphors and idioms involving head. The meanings of these phrases go beyond the literal translations of the words.

Let's backtrack a bit. First, let me pay you a compliment for reading this column. Since I don't know you, I'll use the polite form *vy: Vy máte hlavu!* Of course "you have a head," but I'm really telling you that you're smart. We know that language is sexist, so only a woman would say, *Dám si udělat hlavu,* "I'll have my head done," when she's going to have her hair done. Male or female, however, surely "you wash your head," *myjete si hlavu,* when you shampoo. But if I wanted to wash your brain, I'd say, *Blbnout vám hlavu,* that is, "Make your head crazy."

I hope this makes sense, which in Czech is *má to hlavu a patu,* "it has a head and a heel". And if you want to know Czech well, you can't ignore grammar, *házet gramatiku za hlavu* — literally, "Throw grammar behind your head." If you've "had it" for now, don't be afraid to say: M*ám toho až nad hlavu,* "I have it above my head."

Czech Prevails Over Foreign Pressures

Where does Czech come from? Like its country, the Czech language has an impressive history — troubled, but victorious in the end.

As a member of the Indo-European group, Czech shares an origin with English, German, French and most other European languages. By the sixth century, a language called Old Slavonic was spoken in the region inhabited by the ancient Slavic tribes. Traces of Czech can be found in its written form, Old Church Slavonic, which was brought along with Christianity to Moravia in the ninth century by the Greek priests Cyril and Methodius. The use of Old Church Slavonic as the ecclesiastical and literary language spread to Bohemia, where it was used along with Latin — the universal language of medieval Europe — until the 13th century.

Under Charles IV, Holy Roman Emperor and patron of the arts and education, the prosperous kingdom of Bohemia witnessed a revival of Czech. Outstanding documents from this period are *Dalimilova Kronika*, "Dalimil's Chronicle," and *Legenda svaté Kateřiny*, "St. Catherine's Legend." The first printed book in Czech was *Kronika trojanká*, "Trojan Chronicle," which was published in Plzeň in 1468.

But the social and religious upheavals during the Hussite wars brought a decline in the official use of Czech. And the defeat of the Czech patriots at the Battle of White Mountain in 1620 caused the language to stagnate. Latin took over, then was gradually replaced by German.

After 1774, German became the language of instruction in Czech schools. A new wave of Czech revivalism began soon after, and a century later the Czech tongue was strong enough to compete with German in public spheres.

With the political changes of the 20th century, Czech has yielded to the influences of German, Russian and currently English. So don't be surprised to find many foreign words in today's Czech — they're a small reminder of its complex history.

Going Crazy With Czech Motion Verbs

Before you set out on a trip, you must know where, how, and when you going before you can select a Czech verb. If your journey is determinate — a one-time trip with a known destination — and you're going on foot or using transportation to go somewhere within the city, you're "walking": *jdete* from the infinitive *jít*. If you're traveling a long distance, by car, bus or bicycle, for instance, you're "going": *jedete*, from the infinitive *jet*.

Logic might suggest that the verb *jít*, the "walking" verb, would only be used to express going somewhere by foot. But Czechs, like other Slavs, hold that when you go to certain nearby events and places, you "walk," regardless of whether or not you use a vehicle to get there. Say *Jdu na koncert*, " I'm going to a concert," rather than *Jedu na koncert,* which emphasizes your "riding" ability (perhaps you've got a new car).

If your "going" takes place in the future, use the prefix *pů-* for the "walking" verb or *po-* for the "going" verb. For example, "I'll go to work" is *Půjdu do práce* —going to work is a form of "walking" — but *Pojedu do New Yorku* (a long distance), "I'll go to New York." Remember, you can't walk to Brno, Budapest or New York —you can only *jet*.

"Walking" and "going" verbs have no infinitive in the future tense. Any attempt to create one by putting the prefix together with the present-tense infinitive — *pojít* or *pojet* —would be a vaste of energy and even subjet to ridicule, for *pojít* means "to die," applied usually to animals, not people.

There is, however, a whole range of prefixes you can attach to the infinitive *jít*: *přijít*, "to come," *přejít*, "to cross," *vejít*, "to enter," *zajít*, "to stop by," and many others, but they all, as the examples show, change the meaning of *jít*.

And what if you're less determined in your destination, or you go there regularly? No problem. Czech has a verb for it: the non-determinate "walking" verb *chodit* or the "going" verb *jezdit*. Try *Chodím po Praze*, "I walk around Prague," or *Jezdím po městě*, "I ride around the city," and you'll get there. Believe me.

A *Žumpa* By Any Other Name...

In this day and age we take surnames for granted, but there was a time when people didn't have them. In those days, only first names were used to record marriages, births and the like. People often had identifying tags tacked on, however, referring to their personal characteristics, trade, village or house. This could lead to fathers, sons and brothers having different last names: In one case, Jan *řečený Pštros,* "John called Ostrich," was the son of Vaněk *Zlý bečvář,* "Vaněk the Evil Barrel Maker." A 16th-century record shows that the brother of Augustin *Větrovský* (from *vítr,* "wind") was called Šimon *Vorel* (from *vorel/orel,* "eagle").

It was customary to give a trade name to a young man after he had finished his apprenticeship. Many of surviving Czech family names have this origin: *Havíř,* "Miner;" *Hli~ák,* from *hlína,* "earth," for a man who dug earth in mines; *Štola,* a mine passage; *Řezník,* "Butcher;" *Žumpa,* "Sewer;" *Želízko,* a diminutive for someone who worked with *železo,* "iron;" *Krejčí,* "Tailor."

Odd names such as *Skočdopole,* "Jump in the Field," *Kratochvíl,* "Diversion;" *Jelínek,* "Little Deer," and *Karafiát,* "Carnation," were recorded in the 18th century. Children were often named after their father — or their mother if she was unmarried — but orphans received a variety of surnames: *Lipenský* after the town of Lipník; *Bezejmenný,* "Without a Name;" *Nalezený,* "Found;" or *Nevinný,* "Innocent."

In the 15th and 16th centuries, women often kept their own names referring to their home towns or family property, or combined them with their husbands' names: *Anna z Rožmitála,* "from Rožmitál;" *Voršila čertová, rodilá z Krumlova,* "Voršila the Devil, born in Krumlov;" *Dorota Chřenová, někdy Mikuláše Zlenického z Zlenic,* "Dorota the Horseradish, sometimes called a wife of Mikuláš Zlenický from Zlenice." Over a period of centuries, some names — especially the foreign ones —were distorted: the Polish *Czesaný* "Brushed" became the Czech *česaný* only in the last century. Also it was not uncommon for a man to be called after his wife. *Studnička,* "Little Well," is one of these wife-surnames.

In 1780, the Hapsburg Emperor Josef II issued a decree demanding that his subjects have a family name. It was not until the 19th century, however, that many Czech names acquired regular grammatical forms — and family names gelled into today's spellings. The old nickname *Dobředělej,* "Do well," took an adjectival ending and became *Dobředělý* — as good a name as any.

A *Mapa* to **Common Roots**

If something becomes a constant annoyance to you, you may say it's a thorn in your side. In Czech, you talk about a "thorn in your eye," *trn v oku*. *Trn* is an intriguing word, not only because it has no vowels, but because it shares a common, Indo-European origin with the English word "thorn." The "th" in many English words, often of Latin and Greek origin, is rendered in Czech as "t," as in "theme," *téma;* "theology," *teologie*.

There are many words that you may recognize once you realize that Czech and English, along with many European languages, have a common progenitor. Just look at words denoting family relationships: *bratr,* "brother;" *sestra,* "sister;" *matka,* "mother;" and *fotr,* a slang word for "father."

A number of nouns fall into this category that you can view as "common origin — common sense." Some are easily recognizable, such as *mapa,* "map," and *karta,* "card" and *papír,* "paper"; others require some imagination to see the connection: *klíč,* "key," *kuchyň,* "kitchen," *mléko* and its spoken equivalent *mlíko,* "milk." Still others have changed their meanings with time: *list,* "leaf" or "sheet," versus the English "list"; *stůl,* "table," versus English "stool."

Now, without knowing Czech, you surely can recognize words of Latin and Greek origins, such as *túra, turista, auto, autobus, víkend, byznys, fax, biologie, matematika,* and many others. So don't say you don't know any Czech!

Getting Hooked on the Soft "N"

The Czech letter *ň* can cause complications, not so much in its pronunciation as in its graphic presentation, and in its presence in pronouns.

The sound *ň,* or "palatal (soft) *n,* "is similar to the first *n* in the English "onion." The *háček,* or "hook," doesn't always reside on the *n,* however. When *ň* is followed by *-e,* the *háček* shifts to the *-e,* as in *někdo,* "somebody." But remember that the *háček* affects the pronunciation of the *n,* not the *e.* When you see the combination *ne* without any *háček,* however, simply say it the usual way: *nebe,* "sky," *konec,* "end," *poledne,* "noon." On the other hand, when followed by *i* or *í, n* always inherits the quality of *ň,* as in *nikdo,* "no one," and *podnik,* "enterprise." This is reasonable, because Czech is a logical language: *ň* is really nothing but a soft *n,* and the *měkké -i,* or soft *-i,* makes the *-n* soft too.

To see how this works in the real language, think of him, her and them. These personal pronouns (in the nominative *on,* "he," *ona,* "she" and *oni,* "they") need their proper forms in each case. After a preposition, though, these pronouns (and also the neuter *ono,* "it") always begin with the sound *ň.* Take, for example, the sentence *Nerozumím jemu, ale rozumím jí a jim,* "I don't understand him, but I understand her and them." The pronouns are in the dative, but if you put a preposition in front of that case, you'd get the forms in *ň: Jdu k němu, ale nejdu k ní nebo k nim.* "I'm going to him, but not to her or to them." While it's true that there are short forms of these pronouns, such as *mu* (instead of *jemu*), *ho* (instead of *jeho*), the forms with *ň* after prepositions are a must. Softly, softly with third-person pronouns after prepositions. Remember, there are no shortcuts in Czech!

Tracing Names' Histories

The town of Pilsen — in Czech, *Plzeň* — is associated with beer, but have you ever thought about where its name comes from? According to etymologists Josef Holub and František Kopečný, the origin of the word *plzeň* goes back to *plazit*, "crawl," and *plž*, "slug" — not very appetizing to consider while drinking your *Plzeňské pivo*, or Pilsner beer. While some Czech place names are of obscure origin, others are quite evocative. The name *Dobřichovice* is compounded of *břicho*, "belly," with the preposition *do*, "in, into," and the ending *-ice* (frequently denoting place names). Put them together to get "Into the Belly Town." Known in the past as a summer retreat of Prague's well-to-do, the town has little connection with bellies. Nearby *Řevnice*, known for the tennis courts where Martina Navrátilová used to hit the ball as a child, has *řev*, "roar, roaring" in its stem; call it "Roaring Town."

Karlovy Vary, on the other hand, makes a lot of sense. Named after Charles IV, the town has boiling springs and, indeed, *Vary* comes from the word *vřít*, "boil." *Mydlovary*, similarly, denotes a place where *mýdlo*, "soap" was made or "boiled."

The *Šumava*, hills covered by scented forests, got their name from *šumět*, "hum" — the "Humming Hills." The suffix *-čany* is common in Czech place names and means "site." *Hradčany* is "Castle Site," (*hrad* means "castle"), and the Prague neighborhood of *Vysočany* means "The High Site," from *vysoký*, "high, tall."

Děvín hill in Prague 5 has its origin in old Slavic *div*, "marvel, wonder, spirit." You could translate it as "Site of Women Fighters," because some etymologists believe it was named after *děvy*, fierce women of ancient times. Conversely, some town names suggest unfriendly inhabitants: *Vráž* apparently comes from *nevraživý*, "spiteful, malicious," and there surely is more than one Vráž. But I'll bet you could find many villages embracing in their names words like *dobrý*, "good," and *srdce*, "heart."

Been Having *Lots* of Problems

Those were the days! You used to sleep well, have a lot of friends and a lot of fun. If you want to speak about those good old days in Czech, you can use special verbal forms called frequentatives. For instance, with the verb "to be," using the past tense of the frequentative *bývávat* is enough to express your longing for those fabulous days.

When you listen carefully to old folks, you may notice that they use a variety of these *-ávat* and *-ívat* verbal forms, not only in the past, but also in the present.

You don't necessarily have to be old to use these frequentatives, but you must feel old enough to have gone through an experience of fairly regular activity, such as having problems, seeing movies, reading newspapers, etc.

If you wanted to connect these three examples together, you could say in Czech, exactly as in English: *Když mám problém, chodím do kina nebo čtu noviny* — "When I have a problem, I go to the cinema or read newspapers." Or you may prefer to sound like a well-experienced person and say: *Když mívám problém, chodívám do kina nebo čítávám noviny*, using the frequentatives of *mít, chodit* and *číst* to express the recurrence of your problems and your solutions.

Using one form rather than the other basically makes no difference. The choice depends on your style — in life and in speech.

A New Year's Card With Heart

Czech New Year's greeting cards tend to be straightforward. Most of them bear the classic message *Radostné vánoce a šťastný nový rok,* "Merry Christmas and Happy New Year." While English-speaking well-wishers are flexible in offering a variety of greetings from "Best Wishes for a year of peace and love" to ones with a religious message, Czechs limit their greetings to a few traditional favorites.

Being immensely proud of their history, Czechs love cards with pictures of Prague Castle, St. Nicholas cathedral and other historical/tourist attractions. These cards typically read *Novoroční pozdrav z Prahy* with English, German and French translations.

The adjectival expression *novoroční* comes from *nový rok,* "New Year," and can be attached to any greeting, such as *pozdrav,* "greetings, regards" or *přání,* "wishes."

Czechs glorify *srdce,* "heart," as a center of warmth, and one can preface almost any greeting with its adjectival form, *srdečný.* Thus, *Srdečné přání k novému roku,* literally meaning "Cordial wishes for the New Year," is not uncommon on New Year's greeting cards. It is, however, important to distinguish between *srdečný,* "cordial, hearty," and *srdeční,* "cardiac"!

If you receive a *P.F.* greeting card, don't speculate what its inscription means. The abbreviation *P.F.* comes from French *pour félicité,* "for supreme happiness," and this sort of New Year cards is popular particularly among artists and intellectuals.

A Preposition for All Reasons

Imagine an American, in his early 30s, interested in meeting a Czech girl. For this purpose, he puts an ad in a Czech newspaper: *Hledám dívku na dopisování*, "I'm looking for a girl to correspond with." After describing himself in romantic terms, he becomes more practical, revealing his assets: *Mám dům na bydlení...*, "I have a house to live in...," *chatu na léto...*, "a summer cottage...," *auto na všední dny...*, "one car for daily usage...," *auto na výlety*, "another car for trips." However, he doesn't have *paní na uklízení*, "a cleaning lady" — he does his domestic choirs himself: he washes dishes in *myčka na nádobí*, "a diswasher," and does laundry in *pračka na praní*, "a washer," drying his clothes in *sušička na prádlo*, "a dryer."

A romantic at heart, the fellow promises to bring *kytici na setkání*, "a bouquet at their first meeting," and to take the girl out for a *přípitek na zdraví a na známost*, "a toast to their health and acquaintance." But before all this happens, he wants the girl to send him *foto na památku*, her "photo as a memento." Of course, only if he likes her picture will he pack his *kufry na cestování*, "suitcases for travel," and head to meet her in golden Prague.

This guy may sound like a nerd, but he really isn't. He's a man with a purpose — just like all those words taking a preposition *na* to express a reason or purpose. He's currently studying Czech, and is *zralý na ženění*, "ready for marriage," and due to his Czech ancestry, he's looking for a Czech *dívka na vdávání*, "girl to wed." Is someone there, in the old country, interested?

Try Not To Throw Tantum Tantrums

They come in pairs, or they come alone — the so-called Pluralia Tantum. Less esoteric than their collective title suggests, they are the words that have no singular, and thus exist only in the plural. As in English, they come in pairs as garments (*kalhoty,* "pants," and *šortky,* "shorts"), as parts of the human body (*plíce,* "lungs"), and as everyday objects (*brýle,* "glasses," and *nůžky,* "scissors").

Their category is larger in Czech than in English. Let's look at the plural nouns that sound less natural to English speakers because they exist in English in both numbers.

Peníze, "money" comes from a little-used singular word *peníz,* "coin," which may be related to English "penny." Grammatically, *peníze* declines as a soft masculine noun, except for the genitive, which is *peněz,* a feminine form. *Hodinky,* "a watch," and *hodiny,* "a clock" are also known in the plural only. To be sure, there are singular forms *hodinka,* "a little hour," and *hodina,* "an hour," but as the English equivalents indicate, they have different meanings. *Šaty,* "dress," in spoken Czech also "men's suit," has the masculine declension (the singular *šat,* "garment" is an obsolete form).

Pluralia Tantum can be categorized, but they have no particular points in common to help you identify them. Two words, *vánoce,* "Christmas," and *velikonoce,* "Easter," fall into a religious-holidays category and also belong to the grammatical group of soft feminine nouns. From the viewpoint of grammar, we could add here *prázdniny,* "vacation" and also the names of certain towns and districts, such as *Budějovice,* known for its brewery; *Řevnice,* where Martina Navrátilová comes from; *Dobřichovice,* a town near Prague where the writer Ludvík Vaculík has a cottage, and *Dejvice,* a well-known district in Prague 6.

With geographical names, we find many other Pluralia Tantum: *Karlovy Vary, Klatovy, Čechy* (Bohemia), *Hradčany* (Prague Castle), etc. They tend to have feminine gender.

You may ask why *noviny,* "a newspaper," *dveře,* "a door," and *záda,* "back (of a body)" have no singular. In the same way, a Czech might wonder why English has "hair," *vlasy* in the singular only. Don't we have more than one hair on our heads? But let's give some credit to our ancestors — sometimes they were a little illogical, like ourselves.

Not All Theresa's Fruits were Bitter

If the word *Terezín* brings to mind only images of the ghetto where the Nazis herded Jews before shipping them off to death camps, remember that the town also had a rich, if not exactly happy, history before World War II. Built between 1780 and 1790 by Emperor Josef II as a fortress, the complex could accomodate as many as 10,000 soldiers. This world of its own, called *Theresienstadt* in German, boasted bakeries, mills, factories and prisons. Both the 1848 revolutionary year and the assassination of the imperial successor to the Austro-Hungarian throne, Archduke František Ferdinand, in 1914 brought prisoners to *Terezín*. As the name suggests, Josef II named the fortress after his mother, Maria Theresa, Empress of Austria — and hence Queen of Bohemia — from 1740 to 1780.

Maria Theresa was a progressive ruler with a strong will — aside from delivering 16 children (many of whom enlarged the power of the Austrian monarchy through their marriages), she worked to improve education and develop industry, including Bohemia's glass factories, with the idea of strengthening her state.

Her second name — *Tereza* in Czech — comes from the Greek, where it means "reaper." It's a common name in Czech culture, with its name day on October 15. A leading character in recent Czech literature — the troubled, dependent wife in Milan Kundera's *Unbearable Lightness of Being* — is named *Tereza*. As for the town of Terezín, its place in Czech life during the Nazi occupation has been the subject of much serious literature, for example, *Terezínské Requiem*, "The Terezín Requiem" by Josef Bor. Arnošt Lustig and Ivan Klíma have also drawn on their personal experiences in the ghetto for their fiction. The well-known playwright Pavel Kohout set his novel *Hodina tance a lásky*, "A Dance and Love Lesson," in Terezín, but told from the point of view of the Nazi commander, which, as is hardly surprising imagine, evoked a great deal of bitter criticism.

In any case, when you hear "Terezín," don't think just of its grim history, but also of the enlightened Empress Maria Teresa.

Adverbs: Up, Up and Away

"Up and down, to the right and to the left!" If this sounds to you like an exercise session with Jane Fonda, you would translate it into Czech using adverbs denoting motion: *Nahoru a dolů, doprava a doleva!* If you perceive the phrase as referring to something being located up and down, on the right and on the left, you would use *Nahoře a dole, doprava a doleva*. If you need to take something from above, below, the right or the left, say: *Shora a zdola, zprava a zleva*. Non-native speakers must learn to see their surroundings as either at rest or in motion. Thus, *Jsem doma* means "I'm at home," *Jdu domů,* "I'm going home," and *Jdu z domova,* "I'm coming from home."

The same concept is applied when asking whether someone is located at, going toward or coming from a place: *Kde jsi?* "Where are you?" *Kam jdeš?* "Where are you going?" and *Odkud jdeš?* "From where are you coming?" The same goes for *tady,* "here," *tam,* "there" and *odtamtud,* "from there." *Tady je!* "Here she/he is," *Tam jde!* "There she/he goes," and *Jde odtamtud,* "She's/he's coming from there."

These location and motion words come in trios, one for each English equivalent. It is a good idea to become familiar with at least the basic ones, such as, "outside," *venku/ven/zvenčí;* "inside," *uvnitř (vevnitř)/dovnitř/zevnitř;* "here," *tady/sem/odsud;* "elsewhere," *jinde/jinam/odjinud;* "in front," *vpředu/dopředu/zpředu*. But always bear in mind the basic division: location, motion towards and motion out of or away from. Who ever said Czech was easy?

Say 'Aaah' - In Czech

With the weather getting colder, you may be coming down with something — perhaps a runny nose, or *rýma*. While *rýma* literally means the stuff coming out of your nose, Czech-English dictionaries tend to translate it as "cold in the head." It's quite misleading because when you have a cold, all your body is affected. So, if you need to describe your runny nose to a doctor, say *mám rýmu*.

But if your symptoms are more severe, know that English is less specific than Czech when describing discomfort and pain. For instance, the word *břicho* means "abdomen, belly." While a child might say "my tummy hurts," you may prefer "my stomach aches," even if the pain is centered in your abdomen. Czechs, on the other hand, distinguish very clearly between *žaludek*, "stomach" and *břicho*, "abdomen," since discomfort in either of those parts of the body suggests quite different causes.

When seeing a doctor about a pain in the stomach, the doctor may ask you if you feel you want to *zvracet*, "vomit." But if you are complaining about a bellyache, he would most likely ask you about *průjem*, "diarrhea."

The word *zvracet* can be a tricky one. It is formed from *vracet*, "to return," and the prefix *z-*, meaning "from inside," which describes fairly accurately this symptom of "returning from inside of your stomach." Its perfective-aspect counterpart, *zvrátit*, is used infrequently in this sense; more generally it means to "knock over (chair), turn over (boat), reverse, overrule (a verdict), or upset (plans)." You can also *zvrátit hlavu dozadu*, "throw head backwards," but when you talk about throwing up, use *zvracet* only.

The word "chest" translates into Czech as *hruď*. But when you see a Czech doctor because of pain in the breasts, stop being prudish and say, *"bolí mě na prsou,"* or "my breasts hurt," because Czechs prefer to use *prsa*, "breasts," in this context.

Verb Becomes Tool for Grading Society

The verb *hrabat,* "to rake," has a number of additional meanings, often relating to people's position in society.

Thrifty or stingy people like to *hrabat peníze,* amass as much money as they can. If you're a conceited person, believing that everyone stands below you in talent, looks, etc., you might express this sense of superiority by exclaiming, *Kam se na mě hrabe!* Literary it means, "To what degree he/she is raking to me!"

Hrabat and *hrabat si* also means "to dig." *Hrabat si na svém písečku* is "digging in one's own sand," going about one's own business.

Czech has no equivalent for "movers and shakers," but the same idea can be expressed by adding the prefix *vy-* to *hrabat se: vyhrabat se.* This refers especially to someone who has risen in position and social status above others' expectations. To communicate surprise in the opposite — when someone has performed below expectations — *dohrabat se* can be used.

Most prefixes with *hrabat/hrabat se* have negative connotations. If you leave Prague to live in a dull village, people might describe your existence with *zahrabat se,* indicating that your ambitions and potential "have died."

The verb for a simple physical movement can take on meanings ranging up and down the social scale: some obvious metaphors, others given meaning by the little prefixes attached to the act of raking. So remember the buzzword for movers, shakers as well as losers. Call it a linguistic equality!

On the Ball and in the Groove

Two prepositions meaning "in" or "at" — in Czech, *v* and *na* — are distinct and yet the same. The rule of thumb: Location *inside* is rendered by *v* (*ve* when standing in front of a word beginning with double or triple consonants) and location or motion on a *surface* is expressed by *na*. If you say *Papír je ve stole*, you're talking about paper being "inside" a table, most likely in a drawer. You must use *na* if the paper is on the top of the table.

This concept looks easy, and it is — until you encounter a series of expressions that cannot take *v* despite the logical meaning "inside." For instance, when talking about educational institutions, the preposition *v* is used for any type of school below the high school level. *Jesle*, "day care center," *školka*, "preschool, kindergarten," *škola*, "school," and *učiliště*, "trade school," tend to connect with the preposition *v*: *Sestra je ve škole a bratr je v učilišti*, "Sister is at school and brother is at trade school." To indicate motion into these institutions, *do*, "into" is used.

But if your sister attends high school and your brother college, only *na* is suitable: *Sestra studuje na gymnáziu*, "Sister studies at high school," and *Bratr je na univerzitě*, "Brother is at the university." When going into these schools, either in terms of attending classes or being admitted, *na* is used as well: *Sestra jde na gymnázium*, "Sister is going to high school," and *Bratr chodí na univerzitu*, "Brother attends university."

Some words are used only with *na*: *pošta*, "post-office," *nádraží*, "train station," *letiště*, "airport," *náměstí*, "square," *hodina*, "class," and some others. *Jsem na nádraží*, "I'm at the train station," or *Jsem na hodině češtiny*, "I'm at Czech class," for example.

A performance tends to take *na*: *na koncertě*, "at the concert," *na opeře*, "at the opera," *na hře*, "at the play," but *v divadle*, "at the theatre" because *divadlo* is viewed as a building. It is the exceptions and deviations that make the use of *v* and *na* difficult and often illogical.

Grammar + Grammar = Success

Language is a communication skill, and you won't get anywhere without it. You may be a math genius, but when asked how much one plus one is in a language you don't speak, you may be taken for an idiot. And Czechs know it — that's why they try to learn as many languages as possible. Recently, two 16-year-old Czech students told me that Americans in Prague project an image of being dumb. It bothered them that so many Americans are eager to teach English without even knowing grammar. When it comes to learning Czech, it's true that many Americans seem to assume that a few expressions from a phrase book will enable them to function in the language. Unfortunately, those booklets don't teach you cases, tenses, grammatical number, imperative or any other "tricky" concepts. Based on simplicity and blatant repetition, they certainly don't work well for those who intend to learn Czech.

Simple words such as *dům*, "a house, and *stůl*, "table" become difficult to recognize in forms like *domu* (genitive case) or *stolem* (instrumental case). You need to be quite imaginative to recognize or produce the past tense form *psal/a jsem*, "I wrote," from *píšu*, "I write." Even the word *Praha* may be misleading in the dative and prepositional cases as *Praze*. *Otec*, "father" and the form used to address a father, *otče*, can be hard to recognize as the same word.

Contrary to general belief, Czech isn't difficult to learn; to speak it quite well (at both the everyday and abstract levels) takes as much time as learning English or any other language — about two years. Those who come once or twice a week to a classroom to learn Czech, expecting to know the language within a couple of months, are simply naive. It takes patience and a knowledge of grammar — not only of Czech grammar but also your own. While I cannot agree with the two Czech girls in their judgment on the IQ of Americans in Prague, I can sympathize with their understanding of the importance of grammar.

Goodbye or See Ya?

When do you say *ahoj, čau* and *na shledanou*? Be aware that Czech is more diplomatic than English when saying "goodbye."

In formal situations, *na shledanou* is a must. It literally means "at the next seeing," but don't confuse it with the English "see you." When parting with a friend, *ahoj, čau* and other slang greetings, such as *těbuch, těpic, těpéro, servus* and *měj se* are appropriate.

Pronounced as one word with the stress on *na,* and *sh-,* pronounced as *sch-, na shledanou* is used only on parting, never on meeting a person. If it's late, you can also say *dobrou noc,* "good night."

But only use *dobré ráno,* "good morning," *dobré poledne,* "good noon," *dobré odpoledne,* "good afternoon," or *dobrý den,* "good day," when meeting someone.

On the other hand, *ahoj* — from English nautical "ahoy" — can be used anytime to anyone you are friendly with. It's the most common word of greeting in Czech.

Čau, from Italian, is more common than slang words of Czech origin such as *těbuch* and *těpic.* You could translate *těbuch* as "Good sees you". In writing, you may also find it spelled *těbuh* or *těbůh.* Talking about God, more decent, however, is *sbohem,* "God with you."

Měj se means "Have a good time," and again, it's appropriate among friends. The polite variant *mějte se* can be used with acquaintances.

But don't forget, to avoid embarrassment, use *na shledanou* with anyone but a good friend.

Na shledanou! So long!